allrecipes®.com

tried & true

slow cooker & casserole

top 200 recipes

allrecipes®
.com

tried & true

slow cooker
& casserole

top 200 recipes

Published by Allrecipes.com, Inc.
400 Mercer Street, Suite 302, Seattle, WA 98109
(206) 292-3990

For distribution information, contact Allrecipes.

Printed and bound in Canada.
Third Edition March 2005

Library of Congress Control Numer: 2003105617

10 9 8 7 6 5 4 3 2 1

ISBN 0-9711-7235-8

SERIES EDITOR: Tim Hunt
EDITOR: Syd Carter
FOOD EDITOR: Jennifer Anderson
PRODUCTION MANAGER: Jill Charing
RECIPE EDITORS: Emily Brune, Richard Kozel, Lesley Peterson
CREATIVE DIRECTOR: Yann Oehl
ART DIRECTOR: Jeff Cummings

Cover photograph copyright 2002, TRG Studios

Recipe shown on cover: *Aunt Millie's Broccoli Casserole* (206)

dedication

. . . .

This book is dedicated to each and every one of you
who long to spend less time at the stove and more time
gathered around the table with friends and family.

acknowledgments

The book you are holding is a community cookbook: the recipes within come from the community of cooks who gather online at Allrecipes.com. It is the members of this community, first and foremost, who we would like to thank - anyone that has shared, reviewed, requested, or tried an Allrecipes recipe. The success of the Allrecipes community resides in your experience, enthusiasm, and generosity.

In addition, a huge debt of thanks is owed to the staff of Allrecipes - the people who have dedicated themselves to building a helpful, supportive environment for our community.

table of contents

introduction

We just can't decide which we love more - the casserole or the slow cooker meal. That's why we put them together in this priceless new collection of recipes. At first glance, slow cookers and casseroles may seem like a contradictory pairing: By definition, you've got to plan, assemble, and start simmering slow cooker meals many hours in advance, while you can whip up most casseroles at the end of a long day with only the baking time standing between you and dinner. But their hearts are in the same place; for at the base of it all, these two cooking styles are both about ease and convenience and good hearty meals to feed hungry families. They require minimal attention; they can be prepped ahead of time; they produce a complete meal from a single dish. They are all about function and flavor without fuss.

Casseroles and slow cooker recipes are not just shortcuts to dinner, and they are not a way of cheating or avoiding "real" cooking. On the contrary, they represent home cooking at its homiest, and often, its finest. Casseroles - complete dishes or meals that are baked and served in the same pan - show up in the cuisine of every culture, often tracing back thousands of years. And slow cookers are just a convenient and modern way to do the kind of slow and gentle home-style cooking that use to require your all-day attention.

When we start to name all of the reasons why we think casseroles and slow cooker recipes are the greatest things since sliced bread, we get overwhelmed - and ravenous. We finally managed to narrow it down to the top ten in each category, followed by our favorite hints for these marvelous methods of cooking.

cooking basics

casseroles

top ten reasons why we love casseroles

1. They're an ingenious way to use up leftovers.

2. They travel beautifully.

3. They freeze well.

4. They're perfect for sharing - take them to potlucks, or give them to friends in need of nourishment and comfort.

5. They easily feed a crowd.

6. There are so many shortcuts to make casseroles even easier - from frozen, precooked meat and vegetables to canned soups, even sauces.

7. The recipes are delightfully flexible.

8. You can make them from ingredients that are easy to keep on hand.

9. A complete meal in one pan offers maximum nutrition with minimum dirty dishes.

10. Everyone loves a casserole. And anyone can make one!

Eating officially begins when the first appetizers are served - your selection can set the tone for the meal that follows. The right presentation and garnish can elevate the simplest dip to a stylish hors d'oeuvre sure to please the eye and the palate.

the casserole quick-fix

One of the most popular ways to use up leftovers is to toss them into a casserole. Any manner of leftover rice, potato, or noodle, plus meat or vegetable equals one very tasty meal. Just cut all your ingredients into manageable, bite-size pieces and mix them together with something that will moisten and bind them - i.e., creamy soup, sour cream, eggs, mayonnaise, tomato sauce, cheese, or broth mixed with a little cornstarch. Season to taste and spread the mixture into a casserole dish or a prepared pastry crust. Then shred a little of your favorite cheese over all and bake at about 350 degrees F (175 degrees C) until heated through and lightly browned on top.

freeze!

It's nearly as easy to make two or three casseroles as it is to make one. Freeze the extras to have on hand for a no-time-to-cook night. Don't want to tie up your good baking pans in the freezer? Keep a few disposable aluminum ones on hand for just this purpose. Assemble the casserole and wrap tightly, first in plastic wrap and then aluminum foil. No need to bake before freezing. When you're ready to eat your frozen meal, it's best to let it thaw in the refrigerator for eight hours or so. If you like crunchy toppings, such as breadcrumbs or potato chips, we recommend you add these ingredients before heating. Remove the plastic wrap and bake at 350 degrees F (175 degrees C) for about 30 minutes, or until hot all the way through. If there's no time to thaw first, you will need to double the original cooking time. A casserole will keep in the freezer for up to six months.

trim it down

Admittedly, casseroles have fallen out of favor with the weight- and health-conscious crowd, because a serving of some casseroles can be a wedge of rich, starchy, cheese-covered guilt. Luckily, it's easy to trim the calorie count and step up the nutritional value of almost any casserole recipe around - even those typically laden with high-fat ingredients.

Simply begin by changing the proportions. Use more vegetables, beans, and whole grains, and fewer creamy sauces, cheeses and fatty meats. Next, substitute reduced-fat versions of ingredients like sour cream, mayonnaise, cheese, cream cheese, salad dressing, condensed soups and prepared sauces. Choose the leanest meats, such as skinless chicken breast, pork loin, and beef round; use soy- or tempeh-based meat substitutes; or at least trim all visible fat and skin from whatever cut of meat you're using. Finally, don't forget to season! There's a whole world of spices to be discovered; you can keep the calorie count down low while you send flavor through the roof.

spice it up

A basic casserole recipe is a fantastic jumping-off point for a wide world of ethnic flavors: Use our spicing chart as a guide for adding punch to an old standard recipe, or improvise with brand-new ones of your own!

- **The Italian pantry:** Oregano, flat-leaf parsley, basil, fennel, rosemary, balsamic vinegar, tomatoes, anchovies, olives, sage, capers, pine nuts, prosciutto, Parmesan, mozzarella and ricotta cheese

- **The Chinese pantry:** Soy sauce, plum sauce, black bean sauce, hoisin sauce, sesame oil, sesame seeds, rice wine vinegar, chili paste, five spice powder, ginger, cilantro, green onions, and straw mushrooms

- **The Mexican pantry:** Cumin, chili powder, oregano, cloves, limes, beans, cotija cheese, corn, raisins, cinnamon, cilantro, tomatillos, pumpkin seeds, and peppers

- **The Indian pantry:** Fenugreek, turmeric, coriander, cumin, coconut, ginger, tamarind, cinnamon, coriander, cilantro, cloves, cardamom, and garam masala

slow cookers

top ten reasons why we love slow cookers

1. You can make so many things in them, from soups to pot roasts to fondue.

2. They cook the cheapest cuts of meat to tender succulence.

3. It's nearly impossible to burn anything in a slow cooker.

4. Operating them requires minimal energy.

5. You can convert your favorite stovetop and oven recipes to slow cooker recipes.

6. It's one of the few cooking methods in which you can cut the cooking time in half by turning up the temperature, and still end up with great results.

7. Foods taste better when they've simmered all day long.

8. You can prep everything the previous night, refrigerate the crock, and then simply set it in the cooker and flip the switch before you leave for the day.

9. They keep foods and drinks warm at parties.

10. They stay home and cook all day so *you* don't have to.

convert your favorites

You can adapt many conventional recipes for the slow cooker, particularly any oven or stovetop recipe that has some moisture in it - i.e., water, broth, wine, sauce, and canned soup. As a rule, you should cut all liquid amounts in half when adjusting for the slow cooker. Remember, too, that the low heat setting is approximately 200 degrees F (95 degrees C), and high heat is about 300 degrees F (150 degrees C). For every hour you'd cook something in the oven or on the stove, allow 8 hours on low or 4 hours on high. (When in doubt, turn it on low and leave it all day or overnight.)

getting even

For thorough heat distribution in a slow cooker, there are a few things you should know: For one thing, many vegetables actually take longer to cook than meat, which is why you should always layer your ingredients. Place dense vegetables like carrots, potatoes, and turnips in the bottom and up the sides of the pot, then add the meat and other ingredients. It's best to fill a slow cooker to at least one-half and no more than three-fourths full. Keep the lid on, too; each time you lift for a peek, heat escapes and you'll have to tack on anywhere from 15 to 25 minutes to the cooking time.

meat matters

While you can cook just about any kind of meat in the slow cooker, some are better candidates than others. Chicken on the bone, as well as cheaper, tougher cuts of beef, pork, and lamb will become succulent and fork-tender under the gentle, moist heat of the slow cooker. For maximum flavor and a more appetizing color, start by removing skin from poultry and trimming visible fat from all meats, then coat lightly in flour and brown in a hot skillet before adding to the slow cooker. One type of meat that you should always brown in a skillet before adding it to the crock, though, is ground beef (or, for that matter, any ground meat). If you don't brown it first, it will clump together, turn an unappealing color and add excess grease to the finished dish.

While browning is usually optional, defrosting is not; any frozen meat must be defrosted completely before being added to the pot. Frozen meat will take too long to reach a safe temperature in the gentle heat of the slow cooker.

go easy on the juice

Because slow cookers work at low heat with their lids on, there is minimal liquid lost during cooking. In fact, it may appear that you have even more liquid than you started with. That's because almost all food, especially meats and vegetables, contain water. As they cook, they begin to release that water. With most cooking methods, the water turns to steam and evaporates. But, since the lid is on the slow cooker, there's nowhere for the steam to go; it just collects on the lid and drips back into the food. Bottom line: If you're inventing your own slow cooker recipes or adapting your favorite stovetop and oven recipes for the slow cooker, decrease the amount of liquid.

be nice to the spice

Whole spices such as bay leaves, peppercorns or cinnamon sticks will give slow cooker items a very intense flavor if left in the pot for the entire cooking time, so use them sparingly. Ground spices as well as fresh and dried herbs, on the other hand, can lose much of their flavor if allowed to simmer for several hours in the slow cooker. It's better to add these items during the last two hours of cooking. Dairy products, such as milk, sour cream, and cheese curdle if cooked too long, so wait until the last hour to stir in these items.

sooner or later . . .

The slow cooker is one of the few cooking methods where you can cut the cooking time in half by turning up the temperature, and still get great results. Food will not burn in a slow cooker because it retains moisture so well, and because the heat is so evenly and gently distributed around the sides as well as the bottom of the pot. If something takes 10 hours on the "low" setting, you can safely cook it for 5 hours on the "high" setting with very similar results.

the finishing touches

As your dish nears the end of its cooking time, it's time to add the finishing touches. If there seems to be too much liquid, remove the lid and turn the pot up to high, allowing some of the water to cook out. If you'd like to thicken or enrich the sauce, now is the time to stir in cream, sour cream, shredded cheese, or a slurry of cornstarch and cool liquid. Brighten up the flavors with salt and pepper, lemon juice or vinegar, and maybe a handful of fresh chopped herbs like parsley, basil, or cilantro.

recipe tips

variations on a theme

You may wonder why we have more than one recipe for some items, such as pot roast or tuna casserole or black bean soup. Don't worry - these are far from being duplicate recipes! Some dishes are so popular that our community members share multiple variations of them. In fact, when you visit Allrecipes.com, you'll find that we have dozens of variations on many of your favorite recipes. As we post new versions of a recipe, we may add a Roman numeral to the title to distinguish it (for example, the "Breakfast Casserole II" recipe which appears in this book). There are lots of different ways to approach even the old standards, and in this book you can simmer up your next tender pot roast with a rich onion gravy and plenty of vegetables; douse it with a fiery Tex-Mex spice rub and roll it up in tortillas; or infuse it with Italian seasonings and the zing of pickled pepperoncini then pile it high on grilled sub rolls. Come see us at Allrecipes.com to explore new renditions of all your old favorites.

about the recipes

Half the fun of an Allrecipes recipe is the story behind it - each of our recipes has comments submitted by the contributor to help explain how the recipe came about, what it's like, or how they use it. As the editors of the Allrecipes cookbooks, both online and in print, the staff works hard to preserve the character of the contributed recipe, but also strives to ensure consistency, accuracy, and completeness in the published version and throughout the collection.

all in the timing

At the top right corner of every recipe in the book, you'll find "Preparation," "Cooking," and "Ready In" times. These times are approximate! Depending on how quick you are with a paring knife, whether or not you use precooked meats in your casseroles, exactly how hot your slow cooker runs (and how many times you open the lid to peek), and any number of other factors - you may find that it takes less or more time than what we've estimated. The "Ready In" times will tell you, on average, how much time the recipe takes from start to finish. With a few recipes, this will be slightly longer than the "Preparation" time plus the "Cooking" time. These are recipes that contain intermediate steps that aren't prepping or cooking, such as marinating meat. Refer to the "Ready In" time to know roughly how long you need between opening the book and serving the finished dish to an appreciative crowd.

need help? we're here for you!

Need more information about an unfamiliar ingredient or cooking term, general cooking information, or difficult technique? We've got a whole section of Allrecipes.com dedicated to giving you all the help you need. In our "Cooking Basics" section, you can search for thousands of kitchen terms, follow photo-filled step-by-step tutorials to learn important cooking skills, and browse or search hundreds of articles that will help you decide what to make and teach you how to make it. You can access the "Cooking Basics" section at Allrecipes: **http://allrecipes.com/cb/**

beyond the book

Each of the recipes in this book can be accessed online at Allrecipes.com. The online versions have some handy, whiz-bang features we didn't manage to squeeze into this book. If you'd like to adjust the number of servings for a recipe, view detailed nutritional information, convert the measurements to metric, or email a copy to a friend, it's all just a click away! The online version also includes user reviews that often include variations and handy tips. We've created a special place on Allrecipes.com where you can find any recipe in this book simply by entering its page number. Check it out! **http://allrecipes.com/tnt/slowcookercasserole/page.asp**

your two cents

Once you try a recipe in this book, you can tell the rest of the world all about it. First, locate the recipe on Allrecipes.com (see above). Next, click on the link that says "Add to Recipe Box" (below the recipe's description). Then, follow the instructions to set up a FREE recipe box of your own. Once you've added the recipe to your box, you can rate it on a scale of 1 to 5 stars and share your comments with the millions of other people who use the site. Come tell us what you think!

tried and true

If you'd like to find out more about this book, the recipes, and other Allrecipes "tried and true" cookbooks - join us online at **http://allrecipes.com/tnt/** or send us an email at **tnt@allrecipes.com**

main dish - beef

Take the day off from cooking and let your slow cooker do the work. Come home to the aroma of a succulent beef roast in gravy, savory stew, or a spicy chili. Make it easy on yourself by preparing dishes heaped with flavors ranging from the popular Reuben Sandwich Casserole to the festively spiced Mexican Casserole. Such delights are always a welcoming sight for family and guests.

Rump Roast Au Jus

Submitted by: **Ardith Simon**

Makes: 8 servings

Preparation: 10 minutes

Cooking: 10 hours

Ready In: 10 hours 10 minutes

"This is a wonderful way to do rump roast in the slow cooker. It creates a wonderful juice while it cooks; serve the juice over individual servings of beef. You'll want the cut to be between 4 and 5 pounds."

INGREDIENTS

1 tablespoon ground black pepper

1 tablespoon paprika

2 teaspoons chili powder

1/2 teaspoon celery salt

1/2 teaspoon ground cayenne pepper

1/2 teaspoon garlic powder

1/4 teaspoon mustard powder

1 (4 pound) rump roast

1/2 cup water

DIRECTIONS

1. In a small bowl, mix together black pepper, paprika, chili powder, celery salt, cayenne pepper, garlic powder, and mustard powder. Rub mixture over the surface of the meat. Place roast in a slow cooker, and add 1/2 cup water.

2. Cover, and cook on Low for 8 to 10 hours. When meat is tender and well done, transfer roast to a serving platter. Skim fat from juices, and strain; serve with meat.

Kathy's Roast and Vegetables

Submitted by: **Jaque**

"This roast is made in the slow cooker with the potatoes and carrots. Very easy and delicious."

Makes: 8 servings

Preparation: 25 minutes

Cooking: 8 hours 20 minutes

Ready In: 8 hours 45 minutes

INGREDIENTS

1 (3 pound) bottom round roast

ground black pepper to taste

garlic powder to taste

1 tablespoon vegetable oil

2 (10.75 ounce) cans condensed cream of mushroom soup

1 (1 ounce) package dry onion soup mix

5 carrots, peeled and sliced into 1 inch pieces

6 small new potatoes, halved

DIRECTIONS

1. Season roast with black pepper and garlic powder. In a large pot, heat the oil over medium heat. Brown the roast on all sides for 20 minutes.

2. Mix together the mushroom soup and the onion soup mix in the slow cooker. Place roast into the slow cooker, and arrange carrots and potatoes around the meat.

3. Cover, and cook on Low for 6 to 8 hours, stirring occasionally.

Garlic Top Sirloin Pot Roast

Submitted by: **DontCookMuch**

Makes: 8 servings

Preparation: 30 minutes

Cooking: 6 hours

Ready In: 6 hours 30 minutes

"Top sirloin roast with garlic, potatoes, onions, carrots, and green peppers slow cooked to perfection."

INGREDIENTS

1 teaspoon salt

1 teaspoon freshly ground black pepper

1 teaspoon paprika

1 (3 pound) top sirloin roast

6 cloves garlic, slivered

6 Yukon Gold potatoes, peeled and quartered

4 carrots, cut into 2 inch pieces

2 large sweet onions, peeled and chopped

½ cup water

½ cup beef broth

3 cubes beef bouillon

1 bay leaf

2 large green bell peppers, cut into 2 inch pieces

DIRECTIONS

1. Rub salt, pepper and paprika into the meat. With a small knife, make slits in the roast. Press the garlic slivers into the roast.

2. Place the potatoes, carrots, and onions in a large slow cooker. Place meat on top of the vegetables. Pour in water and beef broth, and add bouillon cubes and bay leaf.

3. Place lid on slow cooker, and cook for 6 hours on High, or 8 hours on Low. During the last half hour of cooking, add the green peppers.

Deli Style Brisket

Submitted by: **Nicki**

Makes: 16 servings

Preparation: 20 minutes

Cooking: 8 hours

Ready In: 8 hours 20 minutes

"My dad used to make this in his deli in New England and it was the menu's top seller. Easy to make in the slow cooker and the best gravy ever!"

INGREDIENTS

4 pounds beef brisket

1 tablespoon garlic powder

¼ cup ketchup

1 large onion, thinly sliced

1 tablespoon all-purpose flour

¼ cup water

DIRECTIONS

1. Place brisket fat side up into slow cooker, sprinkle garlic powder on top and rub ketchup generously into brisket. Add onion slices all around and on top of meat, add enough water to coat the bottom of the cooker.

2. Cook on Low, all day, for the most tender brisket you will ever eat.

3. For gravy, remove brisket from the slow cooker, and increase temperature to High. Mix flour with ¼ cup water, add to pot, and bring to a boil, stirring constantly.

French Dip Sandwiches

Submitted by: **Giselle**

Makes: 10 servings

Preparation: 10 minutes

Cooking: 12 hours

Ready In: 12 hours 10 minutes

"Using a slow cooker to cook the meat to just-right tenderness, you too can serve a true French Dip to all of your friends and family during the cold winter nights! C'est si bon!"

INGREDIENTS

1 (4 pound) boneless beef roast

½ cup soy sauce

1 beef bouillon cube

1 bay leaf

3 whole black peppercorns

1 teaspoon dried rosemary, crushed

1 teaspoon dried thyme

1 teaspoon garlic powder

20 slices French bread

DIRECTIONS

1. Remove and discard all visible fat from the roast. Place trimmed roast in a slow cooker.

2. In a medium bowl, combine soy sauce, bouillon, bay leaf, peppercorns, rosemary, thyme, and garlic powder. Pour mixture over roast, and add enough water to almost cover roast. Cover, and cook on Low heat for 10 to 12 hours, or until meat is very tender.

3. Remove meat from broth, reserving broth. Shred meat with a fork, and distribute on bread for sandwiches. Used reserved broth for dipping.

Pepperoncini Beef

Submitted by: **Joyce**

Makes: 12 servings

Preparation: 10 minutes

Cooking: 8 hours

Ready In: 8 hours 10 minutes

"Roast beef cooked in a slow cooker with garlic and pepperoncini makes a delicious and simple filling for gyro sandwiches. Serve on hoagie rolls with provolone or mozzarella cheese, and your choice of condiments. When making the sandwiches, place meat in rolls, cover with cheese, and zap in a microwave for a few seconds. Don't forget to use the pepperoncini in the sandwiches."

INGREDIENTS

1 (3 pound) beef chuck roast

4 cloves garlic, sliced

1 (16 ounce) jar pepperoncini

DIRECTIONS

1. Make small cuts in roast, and insert garlic slices in cuts. Place roast in the slow cooker, and pour the entire contents of the jar of pepperoncini, including liquid, over meat.

2. Cover, and cook on Low for 6 to 8 hours.

Slow Cooker Italian Beef for Sandwiches

Submitted by: **Maureen**

Makes: 10 servings

Preparation: 15 minutes

Cooking: 12 hours

Ready In: 12 hours 15 minutes

"This makes a sandwich similar to one I used to get at a local restaurant when I lived in a suburb of Chicago. My all time favorite! Serve on crusty rolls with roasted sweet or hot peppers, if desired."

INGREDIENTS

3 cups water

1 teaspoon salt

1 teaspoon ground black pepper

1 teaspoon dried oregano

1 teaspoon dried basil

1 teaspoon onion salt

1 teaspoon dried parsley

1 teaspoon garlic powder

1 bay leaf

1 (.7 ounce) package dry Italian-style salad dressing mix

1 (5 pound) rump roast

DIRECTIONS

1. Combine water with salt, ground black pepper, oregano, basil, onion salt, parsley, garlic powder, bay leaf, and salad dressing mix in a saucepan. Stir well, and bring to a boil.

2. Place roast in slow cooker, and pour salad dressing mixture over the meat.

3. Cover, and cook on Low for 10 to 12 hours, or on High for 4 to 5 hours. When done, remove bay leaf, and shred meat with a fork.

Charley's Slow Cooker Mexican Style Meat

Submitted by: **Charley Bishop**

Makes: 12 servings

Preparation: 30 minutes

Cooking: 10 hours

Ready In: 10 hours 30 minutes

"This recipe can be used with chicken, beef, pork and even venison. It freezes well, and can be made into burritos, tacos, or any number of other Mexican-style dishes. This dish uses a lot of spice, so please be sure to adjust to your taste."

INGREDIENTS

1 (4 pound) chuck roast

1 teaspoon salt

1 teaspoon ground black pepper

2 tablespoons olive oil

1 large onion, chopped

1¼ cups diced green chile pepper

1 teaspoon chili powder

1 teaspoon ground cayenne pepper

1 (5 ounce) bottle hot pepper sauce

1 teaspoon garlic powder

DIRECTIONS

1. Trim the roast of any excess fat, and season with salt and pepper. Heat olive oil in a large skillet over medium-high heat. Place meat in hot skillet, and brown meat quickly on all sides.

2. Transfer the roast to a slow cooker, and sprinkle onion over meat. Season with chile peppers, chili powder, cayenne pepper, hot pepper sauce, and garlic powder. Add enough water to cover ⅓ of the roast.

3. Cover, and cook on High for 6 hours, checking to make sure there is always at least a small amount of liquid in the bottom. Reduce heat to Low, and continue cooking for 2 to 4 hours, or until meat is totally tender and falls apart.

Shredded Beef for Tacos

Submitted by: **Diana Pulliam**

Makes: 16 servings

Preparation: 10 minutes

Cooking: 9 hours

Ready In: 9 hours 10 minutes

"This is the easiest meal you'll ever make. Being a mom of 8 and working, I wanted to find something I can make for dinner with no effort. Start your roast in the morning before going to work it will be done when you get home. You don't even have to defrost the roast. If it is a defrosted roast, put it in around noon, it will be done at 5pm. I've had so many people ask for my recipe, and this is the first time I've let it out of my kitchen. Serve with corn tortillas, lettuce, cheese, and any other toppings you prefer."

INGREDIENTS

1 (4 pound) frozen rump roast

1 cup white wine

2 (7.75 ounce) cans Mexican style hot tomato sauce

3 tablespoons crushed garlic

salt and ground black pepper to taste

1 bunch green onions, chopped

1 cup chopped fresh cilantro

DIRECTIONS

1. Place the frozen roast in the slow cooker. Pour the wine and Mexican style hot tomato sauce over the top. Season with garlic, and salt and pepper to taste.

2. Cover, and cook on Low for 9 hours. When done, the roast should shred easily with a fork. Shred the roast into the juices, and mix in the chopped green onions and cilantro.

Slow Cooker Barbeque

Submitted by: **Brandy**

Makes: 8 servings

Preparation: 10 minutes

Cooking: 9 hours

Ready In: 9 hours 10 minutes

"This is an old recipe my mom used to make for us kids. It is so good it almost melts in your mouth! Serve on sub rolls."

INGREDIENTS

1 (3 pound) boneless chuck roast

1 teaspoon garlic powder

1 teaspoon onion powder

salt and pepper to taste

1 (18 ounce) bottle barbeque sauce

DIRECTIONS

1. Place roast into slow cooker. Sprinkle with garlic powder and onion powder, and season with salt and pepper. Pour barbeque sauce over meat. Cook on Low for 6 to 8 hours.

2. Remove meat from slow cooker, shred, and return to slow cooker. Cook for 1 more hour. Serve hot.

Barbecued Beef

Submitted by: **Corwynn Darkholme**

Makes: 12 servings

Preparation: 20 minutes

Cooking: 10 hours

Ready In: 10 hours 20 minutes

"This dish is zesty and yummy! It is very easy to make, as well as very deserving of 3 exclamation points!!! Spoon meat onto toasted sandwich buns, and top with additional barbecue sauce."

INGREDIENTS

1½ cups ketchup

¼ cup packed brown sugar

¼ cup red wine vinegar

2 tablespoons prepared Dijon-style mustard

2 tablespoons Worcestershire sauce

1 teaspoon liquid smoke flavoring

½ teaspoon salt

¼ teaspoon ground black pepper

¼ teaspoon garlic powder

1 (4 pound) boneless chuck roast

DIRECTIONS

1. In a large bowl, combine ketchup, brown sugar, red wine vinegar, Dijon-style mustard, Worcestershire sauce, and liquid smoke. Stir in salt, pepper, and garlic powder.

2. Place chuck roast in a slow cooker. Pour ketchup mixture over chuck roast. Cover, and cook on Low for 8 to 10 hours.

3. Remove chuck roast from slow cooker, shred with a fork, and return to the slow cooker. Stir meat to evenly coat with sauce. Continue cooking approximately 1 hour.

Slow Cooker Pepper Steak

Submitted by: **Marge**

Makes: 6 servings

Preparation: 20 minutes

Cooking: 4 hours 10 minutes

Ready In: 4 hours 30 minutes

"Very tender and flavorful, this recipe is one of our family's favorites. It's great to make ahead of time in the slow cooker and then serve over rice, egg noodles, or chow mein."

INGREDIENTS

2 pounds beef sirloin, cut into 2 inch strips

garlic powder to taste

3 tablespoons vegetable oil

1 cube beef bouillon

¼ cup hot water

1 tablespoon cornstarch

½ cup chopped onion

2 large green bell peppers, roughly chopped

1 (14.5 ounce) can stewed tomatoes, with liquid

3 tablespoons soy sauce

1 teaspoon white sugar

1 teaspoon salt

DIRECTIONS

1. Sprinkle strips of sirloin with garlic powder to taste. In a large skillet over medium heat, heat the vegetable oil and brown the seasoned beef strips. Transfer to a slow cooker.

2. Mix bouillon cube with hot water until dissolved, then mix in cornstarch until dissolved. Pour into the slow cooker with meat. Stir in onion, green peppers, stewed tomatoes, soy sauce, sugar, and salt.

3. Cover, and cook on High for 3 to 4 hours, or on Low for 6 to 8 hours.

Slow Cooker Tender and Yummy Round Steak

Makes: 6 servings

Preparation: 20 minutes

Cooking: 10 hours

Ready In: 10 hours 20 minutes

Submitted by: **Katy**

"Tender and tasty economical top round or bottom round steak cooked in a rich tasting gravy with vegetables."

INGREDIENTS

3 potatoes, peeled and quartered

1 onion, chopped

6 carrots, peeled and sliced into 1 inch pieces

2 pounds boneless round steak

1 (1 ounce) package dry onion soup mix

1 (10.75 ounce) can condensed cream of mushroom soup

3/4 cup water

DIRECTIONS

1. Place the potatoes, onion, and carrots in slow cooker. Cut steak into six pieces, then place the meat on top of vegetables. In a mixing bowl, combine the soup mix, soup, and water; pour over beef.

2. Cover, and cook on Low for 7 to 10 hours.

Slow Cooker London Broil

Submitted by: **Merri**

Makes: 8 servings

Preparation: 10 minutes

Cooking: 10 hours

Ready In: 10 hours 10 minutes

"The steak is cooked with condensed tomato soup mixed with cream of mushroom soup. Dry onion soup mix is sprinkled over the top. Easy by any standard."

INGREDIENTS

2 pounds flank steak

1 (10.75 ounce) can condensed cream of mushroom soup

1 (10.75 ounce) can condensed tomato soup

1 (1 ounce) package dry onion soup mix

DIRECTIONS

1. Place meat in the bottom of the slow cooker; if necessary, slice meat to make it fit!

2. In a medium bowl, mix together mushroom and tomato soups. Pour mixture over beef. Sprinkle dry onion soup mix over top.

3. Cover, and cook on Low for 8 to 10 hours.

Daria's Slow Cooker Beef Stroganoff

Submitted by: **Daria King**

Makes: 6 servings

Preparation: 15 minutes

Cooking: 8 hours

Ready In: 8 hours 15 minutes

"This is a delicious stroganoff recipe. It's very easy and very tasty, using round steak along with mushrooms, onions, and chives. Try serving it over hot, buttered noodles."

INGREDIENTS

1½ pounds top round steak, cut into strips

salt and pepper to taste

½ onion, chopped

1 (10.75 ounce) can condensed cream of mushroom soup

1 (8 ounce) can canned mushrooms

¼ cup water

1 tablespoon dried chives

1 clove garlic, minced

1 teaspoon Worcestershire sauce

1 cube beef bouillon

¼ cup white wine

1 tablespoon all-purpose flour

1 (16 ounce) container sour cream

½ cup chopped fresh parsley

DIRECTIONS

1. Place the beef in the bottom of a slow cooker, and season with salt and pepper to taste. Place onion on top of beef, and then add mushroom soup, mushrooms, and water. Season with chives, garlic, Worcestershire sauce, and bouillon.

2. In a small bowl, mix together the wine with the flour. Pour over the beef.

3. Cover, and cook on Low for 6 to 7 hours. Stir in the sour cream and parsley, and continue cooking for 1 hour.

Hungarian Goulash II

Submitted by: **Rhonda**

Makes: 6 servings

Preparation: 15 minutes

Cooking: 10 hours 15 minutes

Ready In: 10 hours 30 minutes

"This is a dish that my aunt gave me. It takes awhile to make, but it is worth it. Hope you like it. Serve over spaetzle or rice."

INGREDIENTS

2 pounds beef chuck roast, cubed

1 large onion, diced

½ cup ketchup

2 tablespoons Worcestershire sauce

1 tablespoon brown sugar

2 teaspoons salt

2 teaspoons Hungarian sweet paprika

½ teaspoon dry mustard

1¼ cups water, divided

¼ cup all-purpose flour

DIRECTIONS

1. Place beef in slow cooker, and cover with onion. In a medium bowl, stir together ketchup, Worcestershire sauce, brown sugar, salt, paprika, mustard, and 1 cup water. Pour mixture over beef and onions.

2. Cover, and cook on Low for 9 to 10 hours, or until meat is tender.

3. Mix ¼ cup water with flour to form a paste, and stir into goulash. Cook on High for 10 to 15 minutes, or until sauce thickens.

Cabbage Rolls II

Submitted by: **BJ**

Makes: 6 servings

Preparation: 30 minutes

Cooking: 9 hours

Ready In: 9 hours 30 minutes

"Cabbage leaves stuffed with ground beef, onion and rice, covered in a sweet and tangy tomato sauce and cooked in a slow cooker."

INGREDIENTS

12 leaves cabbage

1 cup cooked white rice

1 egg, beaten

¼ cup milk

¼ cup minced onion

1 pound extra-lean ground beef

1¼ teaspoons salt

1¼ teaspoons ground black pepper

1 (8 ounce) can tomato sauce

1 tablespoon brown sugar

1 tablespoon lemon juice

1 teaspoon Worcestershire sauce

DIRECTIONS

1. Bring a large pot of water to a boil. Boil cabbage leaves 2 minutes; drain.

2. In large bowl, combine cooked rice, egg, milk, onion, ground beef, salt, and pepper. Place about ¼ cup of meat mixture in center of each cabbage leaf, and roll up, tucking in ends. Place rolls in slow cooker.

3. In a small bowl, mix together tomato sauce, brown sugar, lemon juice, and Worcestershire sauce. Pour over cabbage rolls.

4. Cover, and cook on Low 8 to 9 hours.

Slow-Cooked German Short Ribs

Submitted by: **Peggy**

Makes: 6 servings

Preparation: 25 minutes

Cooking: 8 hours 20 minutes

Ready In: 8 hours 45 minutes

"Dust off your slow cooker. This recipe is worth it. I love coming home to a waiting meal!"

INGREDIENTS

2 tablespoons all-purpose flour

1 teaspoon salt

1/8 teaspoon ground black pepper

3 pounds beef short ribs

2 tablespoons olive oil

1 slice onion, sliced

1/2 cup dry red wine

1/2 cup chile sauce

3 tablespoons packed brown sugar

3 tablespoons vinegar

1 tablespoon Worcestershire sauce

1/2 teaspoon dry mustard

1/2 teaspoon chili powder

2 tablespoons all-purpose flour

1/4 cup water

DIRECTIONS

1. In a small bowl, combine 2 tablespoons flour, salt, and pepper. Coat the short ribs with the flour mixture.

2. In a large skillet, heat the olive oil over medium-high heat. Brown short ribs in olive oil.

3. In a slow cooker, combine onions, wine, chile sauce, brown sugar, vinegar, Worcestershire sauce, mustard, and chili powder. Mix thoroughly. Transfer the short ribs from the skillet to the slow cooker.

4. Cover, and cook on Low for 6 to 8 hours.

5. Remove ribs, and turn the slow cooker control to High. Mix the remaining 2 tablespoons of flour with 1/4 cup water, and stir into the sauce. Cook for 10 minutes, or until slightly thickened.

Jeanne's Slow Cooker Spaghetti Sauce

Submitted by: Jeanne Gold

Makes: 12 servings

Preparation: 20 minutes

Cooking: 3 hours 20 minutes

Ready In: 3 hours 40 minutes

"This recipe has many vegetables and three kinds of meat. Most people can't tell it's not all beef and I've been told I ought to market it. This sauce has no acidic after taste, which is frequent with sauces that have tomato and/or bell pepper cooked over long periods of time. This sauce freezes well and can be used for other recipes."

INGREDIENTS

1 (28 ounce) can crushed tomatoes

1 (28 ounce) can diced tomatoes

1 (6 ounce) can tomato paste

1 (10 ounce) can tomato sauce

½ pound turkey kielbasa, chopped

¼ cup extra light olive oil

3 onions, chopped

6 yellow squash, diced

1 small green bell pepper, minced

3 cloves garlic, pressed

½ pound extra lean ground beef

½ pound extra lean ground turkey breast

5 bay leaves

15 whole black peppercorns

1½ teaspoons dried basil

1 teaspoon dried marjoram

2 teaspoons dried thyme

½ teaspoon dried oregano

DIRECTIONS

1. In a slow cooker, combine crushed tomatoes, diced tomatoes, tomato paste, tomato sauce, and kielbasa. Set slow cooker to High.

2. Heat olive oil in a large, deep skillet over medium heat. Cook onions, squash, green pepper, and garlic in oil until onions are translucent. Transfer vegetables to the slow cooker.

3. Place ground beef and ground turkey in a large, deep skillet. Cook over medium-high heat until evenly brown. Drain, crumble finely, and transfer to slow cooker. Season with bay leaves, peppercorns, basil, marjoram, thyme, and oregano.

4. Cover, and cook on High for 2 hours. Remove lid, and cook 1 hour more.

Beef Barley Vegetable Soup

Submitted by: **Margo Collins**

Makes: 10 servings

Preparation: 20 minutes

Cooking: 5 hours 30 minutes

Ready In: 5 hours 50 minutes

"Slow cooker, hearty, easy. Serve with a hearty bread, and enjoy."

INGREDIENTS

1 (3 pound) beef chuck roast

½ cup barley

1 bay leaf

2 tablespoons oil

3 carrots, chopped

3 stalks celery, chopped

1 onion, chopped

1 (16 ounce) package frozen mixed vegetables

4 cups water

4 cubes beef bouillon cube

1 tablespoon white sugar

¼ teaspoon ground black pepper

1 (28 ounce) can chopped stewed tomatoes

salt to taste

ground black pepper to taste

DIRECTIONS

1. In a slow cooker, cook chuck roast until very tender (usually 4 to 5 hours on High, but can vary with different slow cookers). Add barley and bay leaf during the last hour of cooking. Remove meat, and chop into bite-size pieces. Discard bay leaf. Set beef, broth, and barley aside.

2. Heat oil in a large stock pot over medium-high heat. Saute carrots, celery, onion, and frozen mixed vegetables until tender. Add water, beef bouillon cubes, sugar, ¼ teaspoon pepper, chopped stewed tomatoes, and beef/barley mixture. Bring to boil, reduce heat, and simmer 10 to 20 minutes. Season with additional salt and pepper to taste.

Slow Cooker Beef Stew IV

Submitted by: **Rosie T.**

Makes: 12 servings

Preparation: 15 minutes

Cooking: 7 hours

Ready In: 7 hours 15 minutes

"Made this on a snowy winter day; it made the house smell good all day long and our tummies full at the end of the day! Best stew I have ever had."

INGREDIENTS

3 pounds cubed beef stew meat

¼ cup all-purpose flour

½ teaspoon salt, or to taste

3 tablespoons olive oil

1 cup baby carrots

4 large potatoes, cubed

1 tablespoon dried parsley

1 teaspoon ground black pepper

2 cups boiling water

1 (1 ounce) package dry onion soup mix

3 tablespoons butter

3 onions, sliced

¼ cup red wine

¼ cup warm water

2 tablespoons all-purpose flour

DIRECTIONS

1. Place meat in a large plastic bag. Combine ¼ cup flour with ½ teaspoon salt; pour into the bag with the meat, and shake to coat.

2. Heat olive oil in a large skillet over medium-high heat. Add stew meat, and cook until evenly browned on the outside. Transfer to a slow cooker along with the carrots, potatoes, parsley, and pepper. In a small bowl, stir together 2 cups of boiling water and dry soup mix; pour into the slow cooker.

3. In the same skillet, melt butter and saute onions until softened; remove to the slow cooker. Pour red wine into the skillet, and stir to loosen browned bits of food on the bottom. Remove from heat, and pour into the slow cooker.

4. Cover, and cook on High for 30 minutes. Reduce heat to Low, and cook for 6 hours, or until meat is fork tender. In a small bowl or cup, mix together 2 tablespoons flour with ¼ cup warm water. Stir into stew, and cook uncovered for 15 minutes, or until thickened.

Slow Cooker Beef Stew

Submitted by: **Nancy**

Makes: 6 servings

Preparation: 20 minutes

Cooking: 12 hours

Ready In: 12 hours 20 minutes

"A hearty, savory slow cooker stew with potatoes, carrots, celery, broth, herbs and spices. You won't be slow to say 'yum'!"

INGREDIENTS

2 pounds beef stew meat, cut into 1 inch cubes

1/4 cup all-purpose flour

1/2 teaspoon salt

1/2 teaspoon ground black pepper

1 clove garlic, minced

1 bay leaf

1 teaspoon paprika

1 teaspoon Worcestershire sauce

1 onion, chopped

1 1/2 cups beef broth

3 potatoes, diced

4 carrots, sliced

1 stalk celery, chopped

DIRECTIONS

1. Place meat in slow cooker. In a small bowl mix together the flour, salt, and pepper; pour over meat, and stir to coat meat with flour mixture. Stir in the garlic, bay leaf, paprika, Worcestershire sauce, onion, beef broth, potatoes, carrots, and celery.

2. Cover, and cook on Low for 10 to 12 hours, or on High for 4 to 6 hours.

Cozy Cottage Beef Stew

Submitted by: **Cat**

Makes: 8 servings

Preparation: 20 minutes

Cooking: 6 hours

Ready In: 6 hours 20 minutes

"It's a delicious blend of tender beef and vegetables, with just the right amount of thick, flavorful broth to tie everything together. Add a loaf of crusty bread, and you have a perfect meal for on the run (microwaves great!) or for sitting down together and sharing the day's events."

INGREDIENTS

3/4 pound beef stew meat, cut into 1 inch cubes

2 onions, diced

3 cloves garlic, minced

1 large stalk celery, minced

2 carrots, finely chopped

1/4 pound green beans, cut into 1 inch pieces

8 ounces fresh mushrooms, coarsley chopped

3 potatoes, peeled and diced

1 (14.5 ounce) can crushed tomatoes

1 (8 ounce) can tomato sauce

1 bay leaf

1/2 teaspoon ground black pepper

1/2 teaspoon dried thyme

1/4 teaspoon dried marjoram

2 (14.5 ounce) cans fat-free chicken broth

1/2 cup all-purpose flour

2 (10.5 ounce) cans beef consomme

DIRECTIONS

1. In a slow cooker, combine beef, onions, garlic, celery, carrots, green beans, mushrooms, and potatoes. Pour in the tomatoes and tomato sauce. Season with bay leaf, pepper, thyme, and marjoram. Stir together chicken broth and flour. Pour chicken broth mixture and beef consomme into slow cooker, and stir.

2. Cover, and cook on low 6 to 10 hours. Remove bay leaf before serving.

Hearty Beef Stew

Submitted by: **Eiore**

Makes: 4 servings

Preparation: 20 minutes

Cooking: 6 hours

Ready In: 6 hours 20 minutes

"This hearty beef stew will put some meat on your bones. The teriyaki sauce adds a nice zest to the flavor of the stew. The meat comes out moist and tender."

INGREDIENTS

1 pound cubed beef stew meat

¼ cup all-purpose flour

1 tablespoon paprika

salt and pepper to taste

1½ tablespoons teriyaki sauce

1 onion, chopped

3 carrots, sliced

1 stalk celery, sliced

2 potatoes, cubed

½ pound mushrooms, quartered

2 cloves garlic, minced

1 bay leaf

DIRECTIONS

1. Place beef stew meat into a slow cooker. In a small bowl, mix together flour, paprika, salt, and pepper; sprinkle over beef stew meat, stirring to coat. Stir in teriyaki sauce, onion, carrots, celery, potatoes, mushrooms, garlic, and bay leaf.

2. Cover, and cook on Low 6 hours, stirring occasionally.

Mom's Italian Beef Barley Soup

Submitted by: **Elaine**

Makes: 6 servings

Preparation: 10 minutes

Cooking: 5 hours

Ready In: 5 hours 10 minutes

"The best beef barley soup. Thickens with just the barley. Tastes best in the slow cooker. Serve topped with parmesan cheese and with a salad."

INGREDIENTS

2 pounds cubed beef chuck roast

5 cups water

4 cubes beef bouillon, crumbled

1/2 onion, chopped

1 (8 ounce) can tomato sauce

3/4 cup uncooked pearl barley

salt and pepper to taste

DIRECTIONS

1. In a slow cooker, combine beef, water, bouillon, onion, tomato sauce, barley, salt and pepper.

2. Cover, and cook on Low for 5 hours.

Texas Beef Soup

Submitted by: **Kim Richard**

Makes: 6 servings

Preparation: 20 minutes

Cooking: 8 hours

Ready In: 8 hours 20 minutes

"A hearty soup that even your husband will like. My husband, who thinks soups are for sissy's loves this recipe! It's so quick and easy because of using the slow cooker. It's sure to be a family favorite!"

INGREDIENTS

2 tablespoons olive oil

1 pound lean beef stew meat

1 tablespoon seasoning salt, or to taste

1/2 teaspoon ground black pepper

1 small onion, finely chopped

1/2 green bell pepper, finely chopped

2 1/2 cups beef broth

1 (15 ounce) can mixed vegetables

1 (11.5 fl oz) can spicy vegetable juice cocktail

DIRECTIONS

1. Heat the olive oil in a large heavy skillet. Season the stew meat with seasoning salt and pepper. Cook meat in the oil along with onion and bell pepper until browned. Transfer to a slow cooker, and stir in the beef broth.

2. Cook on Low for 6 to 8 hours, or until meat is tender. During the last 30 minutes, stir in the mixed vegetables and vegetable juice cocktail.

Slow Cooker Taco Soup

Submitted by: **Janeen Barlow**

Makes: 8 servings

Preparation: 10 minutes

Cooking: 8 hours

Ready In: 8 hours 10 minutes

"This is a quick, throw together slow cooker soup with a Mexican flair. Teenagers love it. Serve topped with corn chips, shredded Cheddar cheese and a dollop of sour cream. Make sure you adjust the amount of chile peppers if you're sensitive about spicy foods."

INGREDIENTS

1 pound ground beef

1 onion, chopped

1 (16 ounce) can chili beans, with liquid

1 (15 ounce) can kidney beans with liquid

1 (15 ounce) can whole kernel corn, with liquid

1 (8 ounce) can tomato sauce

2 cups water

2 (14.5 ounce) cans peeled and diced tomatoes

1 (4 ounce) can diced green chile peppers

1 (1.25 ounce) package taco seasoning mix

DIRECTIONS

1. In a medium skillet, cook the ground beef until browned over medium heat. Drain, and set aside.

2. Place the ground beef, onion, chili beans, kidney beans, corn, tomato sauce, water, diced tomatoes, green chile peppers, and taco seasoning mix in a slow cooker. Mix to blend, and cook on Low for 8 hours.

The Ultimate Chili

Submitted by: **Wendy**

Makes: 6 servings

Preparation: 10 minutes

Cooking: 6 hours 10 minutes

Ready In: 6 hours 20 minutes

"Easy recipe with little preparation time. This can also be made with ground turkey, and it tastes even better the next day!"

INGREDIENTS

1 pound lean ground beef

salt and pepper to taste

3 (15 ounce) cans dark red kidney beans

3 (14.5 ounce) cans Mexican-style stewed tomatoes

2 stalks celery, chopped

1 red bell pepper, chopped

1/4 cup red wine vinegar

2 tablespoons chili powder

1 teaspoon ground cumin

1 teaspoon dried parsley

1 teaspoon dried basil

1 dash Worcestershire sauce

1/2 cup red wine

DIRECTIONS

1. In a large skillet over medium-high heat, cook ground beef until evenly browned. Drain off grease, and season to taste with salt and pepper.

2. In a slow cooker, combine the cooked beef, kidney beans, tomatoes, celery, red bell pepper, and red wine vinegar. Season with chili powder, cumin, parsley, basil, and Worcestershire sauce. Stir to distribute ingredients evenly.

3. Cook on High for 6 hours, or on Low for 8 hours. Pour in the wine during the last 2 hours.

Atomic Canuck Chili

Submitted by: **Mike Purll**

Makes: 10 servings

Preparation: 30 minutes

Cooking: 5 hours

Ready In: 5 hours 30 minutes

"This is a great chili recipe for your slow cooker. It allows you to spice it up as hot as you can take it. Oh, and let's not forget the garlic, eh!"

INGREDIENTS

2 pounds lean ground beef

1/2 large onion, diced

1 tablespoon crushed red pepper

3 tablespoons garlic powder

1 tablespoon seasoned pepper

2 (4 ounce) cans mushroom pieces, drained

1 (28 ounce) can baked beans

2 (15.25 ounce) cans kidney beans with liquid

2 (6 ounce) cans tomato paste

1/4 cup white sugar

3 carrots, sliced

3 stalks celery, sliced

1 green bell pepper, diced

1 red bell pepper, diced

2 jalapeno chile peppers, diced

1/4 cup Canadian beer

2 tablespoons crushed red pepper

hot sauce

1/4 cup barbeque sauce

DIRECTIONS

1. In a large skillet over medium heat, brown ground beef together with onion, crushed red pepper, garlic powder, and seasoned pepper. Drain off the fat, and place the mixture into a slow cooker.

2. Stir mushrooms, baked beans, kidney beans with liquid, tomato paste, sugar, carrots, celery, peppers, beer, and barbeque sauce into the slow cooker. Season with hot sauce and more crushed red pepper.

3. Cover, and cook on Low for 4 to 5 hours.

Slow Cooker Bean Casserole AKA Sweet Chili

Submitted by: **Don Kunesch**

Makes: 6 servings

Preparation: 30 minutes

Cooking: 1 hour

Ready In: 1 hour 30 minutes

"This is a ground beef and pork and bean casserole that my mom used to make. It has a BBQ flavor to it. My kids ask for it twice a week!! Serve with cornbread or brown bread."

INGREDIENTS

½ cup ketchup

¼ cup molasses

1 teaspoon dry mustard

1 (16 ounce) can baked beans with pork

1 teaspoon salt

½ teaspoon ground black pepper

4 slices bacon

1 large green bell pepper, chopped

1½ pounds ground beef

DIRECTIONS

1. In a slow cooker, mix together ketchup, molasses, mustard, pork and beans, salt, and pepper.

2. Cook bacon and bell pepper in a large skillet over medium heat for about 5 to 7 minutes, then add to the slow cooker. In same skillet, brown beef, and stir into the slow cooker.

3. Cover, and cook on High setting for 1 hour.

Baked Ziti IV

Submitted by: **Seth Henderson**

Makes: 12 servings

Preparation: 30 minutes

Cooking: 1 hour

Ready In: 1 hour 30 minutes

"The BEST Baked Ziti!! This has flavor and yields a great amount. Try this recipe; it IS the best!"

INGREDIENTS

1 pound dry ziti pasta

1½ tablespoons olive oil

1 onion, sliced

1 teaspoon minced fresh rosemary

4 cloves garlic, chopped

½ pound ground beef

½ pound ground pork sausage

1½ (26 ounce) jars spaghetti sauce

salt to taste

1 (6 ounce) package provolone cheese, sliced

¾ cup sour cream

¾ cup cottage cheese

1 (6 ounce) package mozzarella cheese, shredded

2 tablespoons freshly grated Parmesan cheese

DIRECTIONS

1. Bring a large pot of lightly salted water to a boil. Cook pasta in boiling water for 8 to 10 minutes, or until al dente; drain.

2. Meanwhile, heat olive oil in large, heavy skillet over medium heat. Cook onion in oil until tender. Stir in rosemary and garlic. Transfer to a small bowl.

3. Place ground beef and sausage in the skillet. Cook over medium-high heat until evenly brown. Stir in the onion mixture and the spaghetti sauce. Season with salt. Reduce heat to low, and simmer for 10 minutes.

4. Preheat oven to 350°F (175°C). Grease a 9x13 inch baking dish. In the prepared dish, layer ½ of the cooked pasta, provolone cheese, sour cream, cottage cheese, and a little less than ½ of the meat mixture. Then layer the rest of the pasta, mozzarella cheese, remaining meat mixture, and Parmesan cheese.

5. Bake in the preheated oven for 20 to 30 minutes, or until heated through and cheeses are melted.

Cavatini II

Submitted by: **Janice**

Makes: 12 servings

Preparation: 30 minutes

Cooking: 1 hour 30 minutes

Ready In: 2 hours 10 minutes

"My Aunt Norma gave me this recipe, and my husband and I love it! Easy to substitute your favorite ingredients like a can of drained black olives."

INGREDIENTS

1 green bell pepper, chopped

1 yellow onion, chopped

2 cups sliced and quartered pepperoni

16 ounces fresh mushrooms, sliced

1 (6 ounce) can tomato paste

1 (32 ounce) jar spaghetti sauce

1 clove garlic, peeled and minced

1 cup rigatoni pasta

1 cup rotini pasta

1 cup macaroni

1 pound ricotta cheese

2 cups shredded mozzarella cheese, divided

¼ cup grated Parmesan cheese

DIRECTIONS

1. In a large saucepan, combine green pepper, onion, pepperoni, mushrooms, tomato paste, spaghetti sauce, and garlic. Cover, and simmer for one hour.

2. Bring a large pot of lightly salted water to a boil. Cook pasta in boiling water for 8 to 10 minutes, or until al dente; drain.

3. Preheat oven to 350°F (175°C).

4. Mix together pasta, ricotta, 1½ cups mozzarella, and Parmesan. In a 9x13 inch baking dish, alternate pasta and cheese mixture and sauce mixture, ending with sauce. Top with remaining mozzarella.

5. Bake in preheated oven for 30 minutes. Let stand for 5 to 10 minutes before serving.

Pasta Bake

Submitted by: **Jodi Beyersdorf**

Makes: 8 servings

Preparation: 15 minutes

Cooking: 40 minutes

Ready In: 55 minutes

"This is my family's favorite dish. Hopefully you already have most of these basic ingredients at home, so you can make it tonight!"

INGREDIENTS

8 ounces mostaccioli pasta

1 pound lean ground beef

1 onion, chopped

1 (4 ounce) can mushrooms, drained

1 (28 ounce) jar spaghetti sauce

2 cups shredded mozzarella cheese

DIRECTIONS

1. Bring a large pot of lightly salted water to a boil. Cook mostaccioli pasta in boiling water for 8 to 10 minutes, or until al dente. Drain well.

2. Meanwhile, cook ground beef and chopped onions in a skillet over medium heat until browned.

3. In a large bowl, mix together the mushrooms, spaghetti sauce, shredded mozzarella cheese, pasta, and browned ground beef and onion mixture. Transfer to a greased, 9x13 inch casserole dish.

4. Bake at 325°F (165°C) for 20 minutes, or until very hot.

Three Cheese Baked Pasta

Submitted by: **Lalena**

Makes: 12 servings

Preparation: 20 minutes

Cooking: 1 hour

Ready In: 1 hour 20 minutes

"This hearty dish always gets rave reviews. Everyone who tries it loves it! Make it a part of your meal today!"

INGREDIENTS

1 pound uncooked pasta

1 pound ground beef

1 onion, chopped

6½ cups tomato pasta sauce

6 ounces provolone cheese, thinly sliced

1½ cups sour cream

6 ounces mozzarella cheese, shredded

½ cup grated Parmesan cheese

DIRECTIONS

1. Bring a large pot of lightly salted water to a boil. Cook pasta in boiling water until al dente. Drain.

2. Meanwhile, cook ground meat and onion in a skillet over medium heat, stirring frequently, until meat is browned. Stir in pasta sauce, reduce heat, and simmer for 15 minutes.

3. Preheat oven to 350°F (175°C). Lightly grease a 9x13 inch baking dish. Layer the ingredients in the prepared baking dish as follows: half of the cooked pasta, all the provolone cheese, all the sour cream, half of the sauce mixture, remaining pasta, mozzarella cheese, and remaining sauce mixture. Top with grated Parmesan cheese.

4. Bake in preheated oven for 30 minutes, or until bubbly.

Baked Fettuccine Lasagna

Submitted by: **Holly**

Makes: 10 servings

Preparation: 20 minutes

Cooking: 1 hour

Ready In: 1 hour 20 minutes

"The fettuccine pasta used in this recipe is a delicious alternative to the typical lasagna noodle. Serve with a green salad and crusty Italian bread."

INGREDIENTS

12 ounces dry fettuccine pasta

1 pound lean ground beef (optional)

1 cup chopped onion

1 cup red bell pepper, chopped

1 tablespoon butter

1 (29 ounce) can diced tomatoes

1 (4 ounce) can sliced mushrooms

3 tablespoons chopped black olives

2 teaspoons dried oregano

1 cup shredded Cheddar cheese

1 cup shredded mozzarella cheese

1 (10.75 ounce) can condensed cream of mushroom soup

¼ cup beef broth

¼ cup grated Parmesan cheese

DIRECTIONS

1. Bring a large pot of lightly salted water to a boil. Cook pasta for 8 to 10 minutes, or until al dente; drain.

2. In a large skillet, brown beef over medium heat. Drain fat from pan, and transfer meat to a bowl. In the same skillet, cook onion and bell pepper in butter until tender. Stir in tomatoes, mushrooms, olives, and beef, and season with oregano. Simmer for 10 minutes.

3. Preheat oven to 350°F (175°C). Lightly grease a 9x13 inch baking dish.

4. Arrange half of the cooked fettuccine in the prepared dish, top with half of the beef and vegetable mixture, and sprinkle with ½ cup of Cheddar cheese and ½ cup of mozzarella cheese. Repeat layers. Mix together soup and beef broth until smooth, and pour over casserole. Sprinkle with Parmesan cheese.

5. Bake in preheated oven for 30 to 35 minutes, or until heated through.

World's Best Lasagna

Submitted by: **John Chandler**

Makes: 12 servings

Preparation: 30 minutes

Cooking: 2 hours 30 minutes

Ready In: 3 hours 15 minutes

"It takes a little work, but it is worth it."

INGREDIENTS

1 pound sweet Italian sausage

3/4 pound lean ground beef

1/2 cup minced onion

2 cloves garlic, crushed

1 (28 ounce) can crushed tomatoes

2 (6 ounce) cans tomato paste

2 (6.5 ounce) cans tomato sauce

1/2 cup water

2 tablespoons white sugar

1 1/2 teaspoons dried basil leaves

1/2 teaspoon fennel seeds

1 teaspoon Italian seasoning

1 tablespoon salt

1/4 teaspoon ground black pepper

4 tablespoons chopped fresh parsley

12 lasagna noodles

16 ounces ricotta cheese

1 egg

1/2 teaspoon salt

3/4 pound mozzarella cheese, sliced

3/4 cup grated Parmesan cheese

DIRECTIONS

1. In a Dutch oven, cook sausage, ground beef, onion, and garlic over medium heat until well browned. Stir in crushed tomatoes, tomato paste, tomato sauce, and water. Season with sugar, basil, fennel seeds, Italian seasoning, 1 tablespoon salt, pepper, and 2 tablespoons parsley. Simmer, covered, for about 1½ hours, stirring occasionally.

2. Bring a large pot of lightly salted water to a boil. Cook lasagna noodles in boiling water for 8 to 10 minutes. In a mixing bowl, combine ricotta cheese with egg, remaining parsley, and ½ teaspoon salt.

3. To assemble, spread 1½ cups of meat sauce in the bottom of a 9x13 inch baking dish. Arrange 6 noodles lengthwise over meat sauce. Spread with one half of the ricotta cheese mixture. Top with a third of mozzarella cheese slices. Spoon 1½ cups meat sauce over mozzarella, and sprinkle with ¼ cup Parmesan cheese. Repeat layers, and top with remaining mozzarella and Parmesan cheese. Cover with foil: to prevent sticking, either spray foil with cooking spray, or make sure the foil does not touch the cheese.

4. Bake at 375°F (190°C) for 25 minutes. Remove foil, and bake an additional 25 minutes. Cool for 15 minutes before serving.

Donna's Lasagna

Submitted by: **Kathy Caswell**

Makes: 12 servings

Preparation: 15 minutes

Cooking: 1 hour 30 minutes

Ready In: 2 hours

"This is a great tasting lasagna, and a family favorite."

INGREDIENTS

1 pound lean ground beef

8 ounces Italian sausage, casings removed

1 (10.75 ounce) can tomato puree

2 (6 ounce) cans tomato paste

2 tablespoons white sugar

1 teaspoon salt

1 clove garlic, minced

1½ tablespoons dried parsley

9 lasagna noodles

3 cups cottage cheese

2 eggs, beaten

½ teaspoon ground black pepper

½ cup grated Parmesan cheese

1½ tablespoons dried parsley

½ teaspoon salt

16 ounces sliced mozzarella cheese

DIRECTIONS

1. Bring a large pot of lightly salted water to a boil. Cook pasta in boiling water for 8 to 10 minutes, or until al dente; drain.

2. Meanwhile, prepare the sauce. In a large pot or Dutch oven, cook ground beef and sausage over medium heat until brown; drain. Stir in tomato puree, tomato paste, sugar, 1 teaspoon salt, garlic, and 1½ tablespoons parsley. Reduce heat, and simmer uncovered for 30 minutes.

3. In a bowl, stir together cottage cheese, eggs, pepper, Parmesan, 1½ tablespoons parsley, and ½ teaspoon salt until blended.

4. Preheat oven to 350°F (175°C). In a 9x13 inch baking dish, layer a third each of the noodles, sliced mozzarella, cottage cheese mixture, and meat sauce. Repeat layers twice.

5. Bake lasagna in the preheated oven for 1 hour, or until hot and bubbly. Let stand 15 minutes before serving.

Reuben Hot Dish

Submitted by: **Sierra**

Makes: 10 servings

Preparation: 20 minutes

Cooking: 1 hour 10 minutes

Ready In: 1 hour 30 minutes

"Sauerkraut, corned beef, Swiss cheese and rye bread - those key Reuben sandwich ingredients, are all present and accounted for in this casserole version of a deli favorite."

INGREDIENTS

2 (10.75 ounce) cans condensed cream of mushroom soup

1½ cups milk

¼ cup finely chopped onion

12 ounces deli sliced corned beef, chopped

3 tablespoons prepared mustard

2 (16 ounce) cans sauerkraut, drained and rinsed

1 (8 ounce) package uncooked egg noodles

2 cups shredded Swiss cheese

2 tablespoons butter, melted

¾ cup cubed rye bread

DIRECTIONS

1. Preheat oven to 250°F (120°C). Arrange bread cubes in a single layer on a baking sheet. Toast until dry. Crush, and reserve. Increase oven temperature to 350°F (175°C).

2. In a medium bowl, mix together the soup, milk, onion, corned beef, and mustard. Set aside.

3. Spread sauerkraut evenly in the bottom of a lightly greased 9x13 inch baking dish. Spread uncooked noodles over sauerkraut. Spoon soup mixture over noodles, and sprinkle with cheese. In a small bowl, mix melted butter with rye bread crumbs, and sprinkle mixture over cheese.

4. Cover, and bake in preheated oven for 50 minutes. Remove cover, and bake an additional 10 minutes.

Italian Meatball Sandwich Casserole

Submitted by: **Holly**

Makes: 5 to 7 servings

Preparation: 30 minutes

Cooking: 50 minutes

Ready In: 1 hour 20 minutes

"All the ingredients for a meatball sandwich are here, just assembled in a different manner. This recipe is always a hit at our house. We NEVER have any leftovers, it is so good!"

INGREDIENTS

⅓ cup chopped green onions

¼ cup Italian seasoned bread crumbs

3 tablespoons grated Parmesan cheese

1 pound ground beef

1 (1 pound) loaf Italian bread, cut into 1 inch cubes

1 (8 ounce) package cream cheese, softened

½ cup mayonnaise

1 teaspoon Italian seasoning

¼ teaspoon freshly ground black pepper

2 cups shredded mozzarella cheese

3 cups spaghetti sauce

1 cup water

2 cloves garlic, minced

DIRECTIONS

1. Preheat oven to 400°F (205°C).

2. Mix together onions, bread crumbs, cheese and ground beef. Roll into 1 inch diameter balls, and place in a baking pan. Bake for 15 to 20 minutes, or until beef is no longer pink. Reduce the oven temperature to 350°F (175°C).

3. Arrange the bread cubes in a single layer in an ungreased 9x13 inch baking dish. Mix together the cream cheese, mayonnaise, Italian seasoning and black pepper until smooth. Spread this mixture over each bread cube. Sprinkle with ½ cup of the grated mozzarella cheese.

4. In a large bowl, mix together spaghetti sauce, water, and garlic. Gently stir in meatballs. Pour over the bread and cheese mixture in the baking pan. Sprinkle the remaining mozzarella cheese evenly over the top.

5. Bake at 350°F (175°C) for 30 minutes, or until heated through.

Ground Beef Shepherd's Pie

Submitted by: **Ginger P.**

Makes: 4 servings

Preparation: 25 minutes

Cooking: 35 minutes

Ready In: 1 hour

"Here's a quick, throw together recipe for shepherd's pie. Browned meat smothered in rich mashed potatoes with your favorite vegetables. A quick and easy dinner to make for your family."

INGREDIENTS

1 tablespoon vegetable oil

1 onion, chopped

1 pound lean ground beef

1 teaspoon dried basil

1 clove garlic, minced

1 cup green beans

1 cup tomatoes, diced

2 potatoes, cooked and mashed

1 egg, beaten

1/2 cup water

1/4 cup shredded Cheddar cheese (optional)

DIRECTIONS

1. Preheat oven to 350 degree°F (175 degree°C). Coat a 2 quart casserole dish with cooking spray.

2. Heat oil in a large skillet over medium heat. Cook onion in oil for 5 minutes, stirring frequently. Stir in the ground beef and basil, and cook and stir for 5 more minutes. Mix in the garlic, green beans, and tomatoes, and simmer for 5 minutes. Transfer beef mixture to prepared dish.

3. In a mixing bowl, mix together the mashed potatoes, egg, and water. Spread evenly over meat mixture.

4. Bake in a preheated oven for 15 to 20 minutes, or until potatoes start to brown on top. Sprinkle with cheese, and continue cooking for 5 minutes.

Easy Mexican Casserole

Submitted by: **Andrea**

Makes: 6 servings

Preparation: 20 minutes

Cooking: 30 minutes

Ready In: 50 minutes

"This is an easy and very tasty dish. I often substitute ground turkey and low fat dairy products and it is still delicious! Serve with chips, salsa and green salad."

INGREDIENTS

1 pound lean ground beef

2 cups salsa

1 (16 ounce) can chili beans, drained

3 cups crushed tortilla chips

2 cups sour cream

1 (2 ounce) can sliced black olives, drained

½ cup chopped green onion

½ cup chopped fresh tomato

2 cups shredded Cheddar cheese

DIRECTIONS

1. Preheat oven to 350°F (175°C).

2. In a large skillet over medium-high heat, cook ground beef until no longer pink. Stir in salsa, reduce heat, and simmer 20 minutes, or until liquid is absorbed. Stir in beans, and heat through.

3. Spray a 9x13 baking dish with cooking spray. Spread crushed tortilla chips in dish, and then spoon beef mixture over chips. Spread sour cream over beef, and sprinkle olives, green onion, and tomato over the sour cream. Top with Cheddar cheese.

4. Bake in preheated oven for 30 minutes, or until hot and bubbly.

Shepherd's Pie

Submitted by: **Sue**

Makes: 8 servings

Preparation: 25 minutes

Cooking: 45 minutes

Ready In: 1 hour 10 minutes

"This isn't the traditional Shepherd's Pie with lamb, but a quick and easy version my family loves."

INGREDIENTS

5 potatoes, peeled and quartered

1 pound lean ground beef

1 (4 ounce) can sliced mushrooms

1 (15 ounce) can mixed vegetables

1 (10.75 ounce) can condensed cream of mushroom soup

1 (10.75 ounce) can condensed cream of celery soup

salt and pepper to taste

3 tablespoons butter

DIRECTIONS

1. Preheat oven to 350°F (175°C). Coat a 9x13 baking dish with cooking spray.

2. Bring a large pot of salted water to a boil. Cook potatoes in boiling water until tender, about 15 minutes. Drain, reserving some of the cooking liquid. Mash potatoes with a little of the cooking liquid. Set aside.

3. In a large skillet, cook ground beef until brown over medium-high heat. Drain fat from pan. Stir in mushrooms, mixed vegetables, mushroom soup, celery soup, and salt and pepper; heat through. Pour into prepared baking dish, cover with mashed potatoes, and dot with butter.

4. Bake in preheated oven for 30 minutes, or until potatoes are golden and beef and vegetable mixture is hot and bubbly.

main dish - pork

Pork comes to us in many flavors, making it the perfect compliment to almost any style of cuisine. Tangy barbequed pork ribs, sweetly simmered roasts that melt in your mouth, lovingly layered lasagnas with Italian sausage, German smoked sausage and sauerkraut stew, or old fashioned pork chops in a creamy mushroom gravy — each recipe will make your dinnertime a special occasion.

Slow Cooker Lancaster County Pork and Sauerkraut

Makes: 6 servings

Preparation: 20 minutes

Cooking: 6 hours

Ready In: 6 hours 20 minutes

Submitted by: **Kathie Boettger**

"Old fashioned pork and sauerkraut that is served here on New Year's Day for luck! Serve with mashed potatoes, and apple sauce for dipping the pork in."

INGREDIENTS

1 (4 pound) pork loin roast

1 teaspoon caraway seeds

salt and pepper to taste

2 cups sauerkraut with liquid

DIRECTIONS

1. Cut pork loin, if necessary, to fit in the slow cooker. Season with caraway seeds, and salt and pepper to taste. Pour sauerkraut over the roast.

2. Cook on High for 1 hour, then cook on Low for 5 to 6 hours. Internal temperature of the roast should be at least 160°F (70°C).

Tangy Slow Cooker Pork Roast

Submitted by: **K**

Makes: 8 servings

Preparation: 10 minutes

Cooking: 8 hours

Ready In: 8 hours 10 minutes

"This recipe is a favorite with my husband. I usually serve it with buttered egg noodles and sugar snap peas."

INGREDIENTS

1 large onion, sliced

2¹/₂ pounds boneless pork loin roast

1 cup hot water

¹/₄ cup white sugar

3 tablespoons red wine vinegar

2 tablespoons soy sauce

1 tablespoon ketchup

¹/₂ teaspoon black pepper

¹/₂ teaspoon salt

¹/₄ teaspoon garlic powder

1 dash hot pepper sauce, or to taste

DIRECTIONS

1. Arrange onion slices evenly over the bottom of the slow cooker, and then place the roast on top of the onion. In a bowl, mix together water, sugar, vinegar, soy sauce, ketchup, black pepper, salt, garlic powder, and hot sauce; pour over roast.

2. Cover, and cook on Low for 6 to 8 hours, or on High for 3 to 4 hours.

Slow Cooker Cranberry Pork

Submitted by: **Dawn**

Makes: 6 servings

Preparation: 10 minutes

Cooking: 4 hours

Ready In: 4 hours 10 minutes

"Sweet, tangy and easy. The sauce is also good with chicken instead of pork. Try serving with rice and onion rings."

INGREDIENTS

1 (16 ounce) can cranberry sauce

1/3 cup French salad dressing

1 onion, sliced

1 (3 pound) boneless pork loin roast

DIRECTIONS

1. In a medium bowl, stir together the cranberry sauce, salad dressing, and onion. Place pork in a slow cooker, and cover with the sauce mixture.

2. Cover, and cook on High for 4 hours, or on Low for 8 hours. Pork is done when the internal temperature has reached 160°F (70°C).

Kalua Pig in a Slow Cooker

Submitted by: **Kay**

Makes: 12 servings

Preparation: 10 minutes

Cooking: 20 hours

Ready In: 20 hours 10 minutes

"This is a simple way of making traditional Hawaiian kalua pig without having to dig a hole in your back yard."

INGREDIENTS

1 (6 pound) pork butt roast

1½ tablespoons Hawaiian sea salt

1 tablespoon liquid smoke flavoring

DIRECTIONS

1. Pierce pork all over with a carving fork. Rub salt then liquid smoke over meat. Place roast in a slow cooker.

2. Cover, and cook on Low for 16 to 20 hours, turning once during cooking time.

3. Remove meat from slow cooker, and shred, adding drippings as needed to moisten.

Sweet Ham Recipe

Submitted by: **Lisa**

Makes: 24 servings

Preparation: 10 minutes

Cooking: 8 hours

Ready In: 8 hours 10 minutes

"A simple and sweet canned ham recipe with pineapple and orange juice. So easy and fantastic!"

INGREDIENTS

1 (7 pound) canned ham

2 cups orange juice

½ cup water

1 (20 ounce) can crushed pineapple

3 tablespoons brown sugar

DIRECTIONS

1. Place ham in the slow cooker. Pour orange juice, water, and pineapple over the top of the ham. Sprinkle brown sugar along the top and sides. Cover, and cook on Low for 8 hours.

Easy Creamy Pork Tenderloin

Submitted by: **Anita Cadenhead**

Makes: 6 servings

Preparation: 10 minutes

Cooking: 8 hours

Ready In: 8 hours 10 minutes

"A very tasty and easy slow cooker pork tenderloin using cream of celery that goes well over rice."

INGREDIENTS

1½ pounds pork tenderloin

ground black pepper to taste

2 (10.75 ounce) cans condensed cream of celery soup

DIRECTIONS

1. Season pork tenderloin with pepper, and place in slow cooker. Pour undiluted celery soup onto tenderloin, covering meat completely.

2. Cover, and cook on Low for 8 hours.

Barbeque Pork Two Ways

Submitted by: **Kimber Maurine**

Makes: 8 servings

Preparation: 15 minutes

Cooking: 8 hours

Ready In: 8 hours 15 minutes

"Easy and Delicious! Pork shoulder, slow cooked or simmered on the stove top with onion and spices. Serve hot in sandwich buns."

INGREDIENTS

2½ pounds pork shoulder

½ cup chopped onion

1 clove garlic, minced

¼ cup brown sugar

1 teaspoon dry mustard

½ teaspoon salt

¼ teaspoon ground black pepper

2 cups ketchup

¼ cup Worcestershire sauce

DIRECTIONS

1. Cut boneless pork shoulder crosswise into ¼ inch slices. Partially freezing it will make slicing easier.

2. In the slow cooker, combine sliced pork, onion, garlic, brown sugar, dry mustard, salt, pepper, ketchup, and Worcestershire sauce; mix well, and cover. Cook on Low, stirring occasionally, for 6 to 8 hours or until the meat is tender. OR In a Dutch oven or large saucepan, combine pork, onion, garlic, brown sugar, dry mustard, salt, pepper, ketchup, and Worcestershire sauce; mix well. Bring to a boil, reduce heat, and cover. Simmer, stirring occasionally, for 2½ to 3 hours or until pork is tender.

Sarge's EZ Pulled Pork BBQ

Submitted by: **Christopher Kruse**

Makes: 8 to 10 servings

Preparation: 10 minutes

Cooking: 8 hours

Ready In: 8 hours 10 minutes

"Too busy to cook? A slow cooker and a can of beef broth gets you started on this recipe. 'Low and slow' cooking gives you a roast that shreds with a fork. As an added bonus you get great stock for beef gravy as a by-product! Serve with your favorite BBQ sauce and plenty of coleslaw."

INGREDIENTS

1 (5 pound) pork butt roast

salt and pepper to taste

1 (14 ounce) can beef broth

¼ cup brewed coffee

DIRECTIONS

1. Cut roast in half. Rub each half with salt and pepper, and place in the slow cooker. Pour broth and coffee over the meat.

2. Turn the slow cooker to Low, and cover. Cook for 6 to 8 hours, or until the roast is fork tender.

3. Carefully remove the roast to a cutting board. Pull the meat off the bone with a fork. You may also chop it with a cleaver afterwards, if you like it really finely cut.

Southwestern Style Chalupas

Submitted by: **Eleta**

Makes: 8 servings

Preparation: 5 minutes

Cooking: 8 hours

Ready In: 8 hours 5 minutes

"This recipe came from my sister who lives in Arizona. It is a very tasty blend of pork, beans and spices served over corn chips. Try topping with cheese, peppers, salsa, sour cream, etc. Everyone who tastes it asks for the recipe. Excellent!"

INGREDIENTS

1 (4 pound) pork roast

1 pound dried pinto beans

1 (4 ounce) can chopped green chile peppers

2 tablespoons chili powder

2 teaspoons cumin seed

1 teaspoon dried oregano

salt and pepper to taste

1 quart water

1 (16 ounce) package corn chips

DIRECTIONS

1. In a slow cooker, combine pork roast, pinto beans, chile peppers, chili powder, cumin seed, oregano, salt, pepper, and water. Cover, and simmer on Low for 4 hours.

2. Shred meat, removing any bones and fat. Cover, and continue cooking for 2 to 4 more hours. Add more water if necessary.

3. Place corn chips on serving plates. Spoon pork mixture over chips, and serve with desired toppings.

Tex-Mex Pork

Submitted by: **Letha**

Makes: 8 servings

Preparation: 20 minutes

Cooking: 10 hours

Ready In: 10 hours 20 minutes

"Mexican style shredded pork. Serve rolled up in tortillas, taco shells or on burger buns with shredded lettuce, diced red onion and sour cream."

INGREDIENTS

1 (8 ounce) can tomato sauce

1 cup barbeque sauce

1 onion, chopped

2 (4 ounce) cans diced green chile peppers

1/4 cup chili powder

1 teaspoon ground cumin

1 teaspoon dried oregano

1/4 teaspoon ground cinnamon

2 1/2 pounds boneless pork loin roast, trimmed

1/2 cup chopped fresh cilantro

DIRECTIONS

1. In a 3 quart or larger slow cooker, mix tomato sauce, barbeque sauce, onion, green chile peppers, chili powder, cumin, oregano, and cinnamon. Place pork in slow cooker, and spoon sauce over to coat the meat.

2. Cover, and cook on Low 8 to 10 hours, or until pork is tender.

3. Remove pork to a cutting board. Using 2 forks, pull meat into shreds. Pour sauce into a serving dish; stir in cilantro and shredded pork.

Amazing Ribs

Submitted by: **Scotty Carreiro**

Makes: 12 servings

Preparation: 30 minutes

Cooking: 4 hours 40 minutes

Ready In: 5 hours 10 minutes

"This is an adapted family recipe. It is a lot of work, but worth the effort. If you do not have a slow cooker, you can bake the ribs for 2 to 3 hours, covered, in the oven."

INGREDIENTS

6 pounds pork baby back ribs

1 pinch black pepper

1 pinch salt

1 pinch crushed red pepper

4 cups barbecue sauce

2 (12 ounce) bottles porter beer, room temperature

DIRECTIONS

1. Cut ribs into small portions of 2 or 3 bones each. Bring a large pot of water to a boil. Season water a pinch each of salt, black pepper, and crushed red pepper to the water. Boil ribs in seasoned water for 20 minutes. Drain, and let the ribs sit for about a half an hour.

2. Meanwhile, preheat an outdoor grill for high heat.

3. Lightly coat the ribs with barbecue sauce. Cook the ribs over high heat for a 5 to 10 minutes on each side to get a nice grilled look to them.

4. Place grilled ribs in a slow cooker. Pour remaining barbecue sauce and one bottle of beer over the ribs; this should cover at least half of the ribs. Cover, and cook on High for 3 hours. Check ribs every hour or so, and add more beer if needed to dilute sauce. Stir to get the ribs on top into the sauce. The ribs are done when the meat is falling off the bone. The ribs were cooked completely in the first process, the rest is about flavor and texture.

Slow Cooker Barbecue Ribs

Submitted by: **Suzanne**

Makes: 8 servings

Preparation: 10 minutes

Cooking: 8 hours 30 minutes

Ready In: 8 hours 40 minutes

"An easy and delicious way to prepare tender barbecued ribs without the barbecue!"

INGREDIENTS

4 pounds pork baby back ribs

salt and pepper to taste

2 cups ketchup

1 cup chili sauce

½ cup packed brown sugar

4 tablespoons vinegar

2 teaspoons dried oregano

2 teaspoons Worcestershire sauce

1 dash hot sauce

DIRECTIONS

1. Preheat oven to 400°F (200°C).

2. Season ribs with salt and pepper. Place in a shallow baking pan. Brown in oven 15 minutes. Turn over, and brown another 15 minutes; drain fat.

3. In a medium bowl, mix together the ketchup, chili sauce, brown sugar, vinegar, oregano, Worcestershire sauce, hot sauce, and salt and pepper. Place ribs in slow cooker. Pour sauce over ribs, and turn to coat.

4. Cover, and cook on Low 6 to 8 hours, or until ribs are tender.

Slow Cooker Country-Style Spareribs

Submitted by: **Julie Maw**

Makes: 8 servings

Preparation: 30 minutes

Cooking: 10 hours

Ready In: 10 hours 30 minutes

"This is an easy slow cooker recipe. This dish ranks as one of my family's favorite Sunday meals. Serve over cooked rice, using sauce as a gravy. My family is picky so I cut the green pepper and celery in larger pieces so I can pick them out before I serve the meal. It doesn't change the flavor, but my kids don't complain about the icky green stuff."

INGREDIENTS

4 pounds pork spareribs

salt and pepper to taste

1 onion, chopped

1 green bell pepper, chopped

2 stalks celery, chopped

2 (8 ounce) cans tomato sauce

3 tablespoons brown sugar

2 tablespoons white wine vinegar

¼ cup lemon juice

2 tablespoons Worcestershire sauce

DIRECTIONS

1. Season ribs with salt and pepper to taste. In a large skillet, over medium-high heat, brown ribs on all sides.

2. Place half of the onion, green pepper, and celery in the bottom of a slow cooker. Place half of the ribs on top the vegetables, then repeat layering with the remaining vegetables and ribs. In a medium bowl, stir together the tomato sauce, brown sugar, vinegar, lemon juice, and Worcestershire sauce. Pour mixture over the top of the ribs.

3. Cover, and cook on High for 1 hour. Reduce to Low, and cook for another 8 to 9 hours.

Slow Cooker Spare Ribs

Submitted by: **Clayton M**

Makes: 4 servings

Preparation: 30 minutes

Cooking: 8 hours 15 minutes

Ready In: 8 hours 45 minutes

"Slow cooked pork spare ribs, or country style ribs, also great with boneless, skinless chicken breasts."

INGREDIENTS

2 pounds pork spareribs

1 (10.75 ounce) can condensed tomato soup

1 onion, chopped

3 cloves garlic, minced

1 tablespoon brown sugar

1 tablespoon Worcestershire sauce

2 tablespoons soy sauce

1 teaspoon cornstarch

¼ cup cold water

DIRECTIONS

1. Place ribs in a large stock pot, and cover with water. Bring to a boil, and cook for 15 minutes.

2. In a mixing bowl, mix together soup, onion, garlic, brown sugar, Worcestershire sauce, and soy sauce. Remove ribs from water, and transfer to a slow cooker. Pour sauce over ribs.

3. Cover, and cook on Low for 6 to 8 hours, or until ribs are tender.

4. If sauce is too thin when cooking time is done, drain sauce from ribs, and pour into a sauce pan. Combine 1 teaspoon cornstarch with a ¼ cup cold water, stir into sauce, and bring sauce to boil. Cook until sauce has reached desired thickness.

BBQ Pork for Sandwiches

Submitted by: **KK**

Makes: 12 servings

Preparation: 15 minutes

Cooking: 4 hours 30 minutes

Ready In: 4 hours 45 minutes

"This is so easy and very tasty. Serve on buns with French fries or potato chips."

INGREDIENTS

1 (14 ounce) can beef broth

3 pounds boneless pork ribs

1 (18 ounce) bottle barbeque sauce

DIRECTIONS

1. Pour can of beef broth into slow cooker, and add boneless pork ribs. Cook on High heat for 4 hours, or until meat shreds easily. Remove meat, and shred with two forks. It will seem that it's not working right away, but it will.

2. Preheat oven to 350°F (175°C). Transfer the shredded pork to a Dutch oven or iron skillet, and stir in barbeque sauce.

3. Bake in the preheated oven for 30 minutes, or until heated through.

Pork Chops to Live For

Submitted by: **Jennifer Johnson**

Makes: 4 servings

Preparation: 15 minutes

Cooking: 5 hours

Ready In: 5 hours 15 minutes

"My mom used to make this all the time and it has always been one of my favorites. The best part is you can mix it up in a few minutes in the morning and forget about it for the rest of the day. You may add an additional can of soup if you want more gravy."

INGREDIENTS

2 tablespoons shortening

4 pork chops

1 egg, beaten

½ cup all-purpose flour

1 large onion, sliced

2 (10.75 ounce) cans condensed cream of mushroom soup

2 cups milk

DIRECTIONS

1. Melt shortening in a large skillet over medium-high heat. Dip pork chops in beaten egg, then dredge in flour. Cook in hot skillet, turning once to brown both sides.

2. Place pork chops into a slow cooker, and arrange sliced onions over meat. Pour soup and milk over the meat and onions.

3. Cover, and cook on High for 4 to 5 hours, or on Low for 8 to 10 hours.

Sour Cream Pork Chops

Submitted by: **Ami**

Makes: 6 servings

Preparation: 15 minutes

Cooking: 8 hours 30 minutes

Ready In: 8 hours 45 minutes

"These are the most tender and succulent pork chops you've ever had. My fiancè absolutely loves them! Serve over noodles or rice."

INGREDIENTS

6 pork chops

salt and pepper to taste

garlic powder to taste

½ cup all-purpose flour

1 large onion, sliced ¼ inch thick

2 cubes chicken bouillon

2 cups boiling water

2 tablespoons all-purpose flour

1 (8 ounce) container sour cream

DIRECTIONS

1. Season pork chops with salt, pepper, and garlic powder, and then dredge in ½ cup flour. In a skillet over medium heat, lightly brown chops in a small amount of oil.

2. Place chops in slow cooker, and top with onion slices. Dissolve bouillon cubes in boiling water and pour over chops. Cover, and cook on Low 7 to 8 hours.

3. Preheat oven to 200°F (95°C).

4. After the chops have cooked, transfer chops to the oven to keep warm. Be careful, the chops are so tender they will fall apart. In a small bowl, blend 2 tablespoons flour with the sour cream; mix into meat juices. Turn slow cooker to High for 15 to 30 minutes, or until sauce is slightly thickened. Serve sauce over pork chops.

Pork Chops a la Slow Cooker

Submitted by: **Jan**

Makes: 4 servings

Preparation: 15 minutes

Cooking: 8 hours 15 minutes

Ready In: 8 hours 30 minutes

"Tender and succulent pork chops coated with spices and browned, then slow cooked in a chicken and mustard sauce."

INGREDIENTS

½ cup all-purpose flour

1 teaspoon dry mustard

1 teaspoon seasoning salt

4 thick cut pork chops

2 tablespoons olive oil

1 (10.5 ounce) can condensed chicken with rice soup

DIRECTIONS

1. In a pie plate or shallow dish, mix flour, dry mustard, and seasoned salt. Trim fat from pork chops.

2. Heat oil in a skillet over medium heat. Dredge chops in flour mixture, then place them in the skillet, and brown both sides.

3. Place chops into a slow cooker, and pour the chicken and rice soup over them. Cover, and cook on Low about 8 hours.

Slow Cooker Chops

Submitted by: **P.J.**

Makes: 4 servings

Preparation: 10 minutes

Cooking: 10 hours 30 minutes

Ready In: 10 hours 40 minutes

"Pork chops in mushroom soup with green beans and tators. Simple, easy and delicious!"

INGREDIENTS

1 (10.75 ounce) can condensed cream of mushroom soup

¼ cup water

1½ pounds boneless pork chops

1 teaspoon ground black pepper

1 (14.5 ounce) can green beans

4 potatoes, peeled and cubed

DIRECTIONS

1. Pour soup into slow cooker. Stir in water to thin soup slightly. Season each pork chop with a dash of pepper, and place chops in slow cooker. Cover, and cook on Low for 7 to 8 hours.

2. Add green beans and potatoes, and cook on High for 2 to 2½ hours. Stir, remove from heat, and serve.

Easiest BBQ Pork Chops

Submitted by: **Janice**

Makes: 6 servings

Preparation: 10 minutes

Cooking: 6 hours

Ready In: 6 hours 10 minutes

"This wonderful little recipe can cook itself in your slow cooker while you're at work. The chops cook up so tender! For all those non-mushroom eaters out there, puree the soup in your blender before adding it to the other ingredients."

INGREDIENTS

1 (10.75 ounce) can condensed cream of mushroom soup

1 cup ketchup

1 tablespoon Worcestershire sauce

½ cup chopped onion

6 pork chops

DIRECTIONS

1. Combine soup, ketchup, Worcestershire sauce, and onions in slow cooker. Add pork chops.

2. Cover, and cook on Low for 6 hours.

Best Italian Sausage Soup

Submitted by: **Perri Pender**

Makes: 8 servings

Preparation: 30 minutes

Cooking: 6 hours

Ready In: 6 hours 30 minutes

"This is one of my favorite soups and it always gets rave reviews! Salad, hard rolls and wine make a meal! You can make this 24 hours ahead of time without the noodles and wait to add the spinach noodles until soup is reheated for serving. Yummy! Serve topped with grated Parmesan!"

INGREDIENTS

1½ pounds sweet Italian sausage

2 cloves garlic, minced

2 small onions, chopped

2 (16 ounce) cans whole peeled tomatoes

1¼ cups dry red wine

5 cups beef broth

½ teaspoon dried basil

½ teaspoon dried oregano

2 zucchini, sliced

1 green bell pepper, chopped

3 tablespoons chopped fresh parsley

1 (16 ounce) package spinach fettuccine pasta

salt and pepper to taste

DIRECTIONS

1. In a large pot, cook sausage over medium heat until brown. Remove with a slotted spoon, and drain on paper towels. Drain fat from pan, reserving 3 tablespoons.

2. Cook garlic and onion in reserved fat for 2 to 3 minutes. Stir in tomatoes, wine, broth, basil, and oregano. Transfer to a slow cooker, and stir in sausage, zucchini, bell pepper, and parsley.

3. Cover, and cook on Low for 4 to 6 hours.

4. Bring a pot of lightly salted water to a boil. Cook pasta in boiling water until al dente, about 7 minutes. Drain water, and add pasta to the slow cooker. Simmer for a few minutes, and season with salt and pepper before serving.

Slow Cooker Kielbasa Stew

Submitted by: **Michele O'Sullivan**

Makes: 8 servings

Preparation: 15 minutes

Cooking: 4 hours

Ready In: 4 hours 15 minutes

"Great flavor and easy to make. Serve with hard rolls, and you have a complete meal."

INGREDIENTS

2 pounds kielbasa sausage, cut into 1 inch pieces

1½ pounds sauerkraut, drained and rinsed

2 Granny Smith apples - peeled, cored and sliced into rings

¾ onion, sliced into rings

2 pounds red potatoes, quartered

1½ cups chicken broth

½ teaspoon caraway seeds

½ cup shredded Swiss cheese

DIRECTIONS

1. Place half the sausage in a slow cooker, and top with the sauerkraut. Cover with the remaining sausage, apples, and onion. Top with the potatoes. Pour chicken broth over all, and sprinkle with caraway seeds.

2. Cover, and cook on High 4 hours, or until potatoes are tender. Top each serving with Swiss cheese.

Sauerkraut Soup II

Submitted by: **Terrilyn Singleton**

Makes: 6 servings
Preparation: 15 minutes
Cooking: 4 hours
Ready In: 4 hours 15 minutes

"This is a wonderful recipe I learned while in college. Serve with a nice crusty bread. You can make this on the stove or in a slow cooker, whichever one fits your lifestyle. Just make sure you have a 4 quart size slow cooker. Note: to make this soup less fattening omit the cream of chicken soup and one of the cans of water."

INGREDIENTS

1 (10.75 ounce) can condensed cream of mushroom soup

1 (10.75 ounce) can condensed cream of chicken soup

2½ cups water

4 cups chicken broth

½ pound sauerkraut

1 onion, finely diced

1 (15 ounce) can carrots, drained

1 (15 ounce) can sliced potatoes, drained

1 pound smoked sausage of your choice, sliced

1 teaspoon dried dill weed

1 teaspoon minced garlic (optional)

salt and pepper to taste

DIRECTIONS

1. In a 4 to 6 quart slow cooker, blend the cream of mushroom soup, cream of chicken soup, water, and chicken broth. Stir in sauerkraut, onion, carrots, potatoes, and sausage. Season with dill and garlic.

2. Cover, and cook on High for 4 hours, or Low for up to 8 hours. Taste, and season with salt and pepper to your liking.

Slow Cooker Split Pea Sausage Soup

Submitted by: **Dorothy**

Makes: 8 servings

Preparation: 20 minutes

Cooking: 5 hours

Ready In: 5 hours 20 minutes

"This is a soup I have come up with myself that everyone in my house will eat."

INGREDIENTS

1 pound dried split peas

10 cups water

1 pound smoked sausage of your choice, sliced

5 cubes chicken bouillon

1½ cups chopped carrot

1 cup chopped celery

2 potatoes, peeled and chopped

½ teaspoon garlic powder

½ teaspoon dried oregano

2 bay leaves

1 onion, chopped

DIRECTIONS

1. In a 5 quart slow cooker, combine the peas, water, sausage, bouillon, carrot, celery, potatoes, garlic powder, oregano, bay leaves, and onion.

2. Cover, and cook on High for 4 to 5 hours. Remove bay leaves before ladling into bowls.

German Lentil Soup

Submitted by: **Claire McLaughlin**

Makes: 8 servings

Preparation: 10 minutes

Cooking: 8 hours

Ready In: 8 hours 10 minutes

"This is a really good lentil soup recipe I created based on the favorite German Lentil Soup which has been served for years at Karl Ratzsch's in Milwaukee. Serves a small crowd, tastes great the next day, and freezes well. Garnish with croutons."

INGREDIENTS

2 cups dried brown lentils, rinsed and drained

3 cups chicken stock

1 bay leaf

1 cup chopped carrots

1 cup chopped celery

1 cup chopped onion

1 cup cooked, cubed ham

1 teaspoon Worcestershire sauce

1/2 teaspoon garlic powder

1/4 teaspoon freshly grated nutmeg

5 drops hot pepper sauce

1/4 teaspoon caraway seed

1/2 teaspoon celery salt

1 tablespoon chopped fresh parsley

1/2 teaspoon ground black pepper

DIRECTIONS

1. Place lentils in a 5 to 6 quart slow cooker. Add chicken stock, bay leaf, carrots, celery, onion, and ham. Season with Worcestershire sauce, garlic powder, nutmeg, hot pepper sauce, caraway seed, celery salt, parsley, and pepper.

2. Cover, and cook on Low for 8 to 10 hours. Remove bay leaf before serving.

Slow Cooker Lentils and Sausage

Submitted by: **Tanya**

Makes: 12 servings

Preparation: 15 minutes

Cooking: 3 hours

Ready In: 3 hours 15 minutes

"A hearty slow cooker meal that is simple to make and satisfying to eat, especially on a cold day! Top each bowl with some grated Parmesan and serve with warm, crusty bread, if desired."

INGREDIENTS

1 (16 ounce) package dry lentils

1 (16 ounce) can diced tomatoes, drained

2 (14 ounce) cans beef broth

3 cups water

1 carrot, chopped

2 pounds kielbasa (Polish) sausage, cut into ½ inch pieces

1 stalk celery, chopped

DIRECTIONS

1. Rinse and drain lentils, but do not soak. In a slow cooker, stir together the lentils, tomatoes, broth, water, carrot, sausage, and celery.

2. Cover, and cook on High for 3 hours, or Low for 6 to 7 hours. Stir well before serving.

Slow Cooker Fifteen Bean Soup

Submitted by: **Joanne**

Makes: 6 servings

Preparation: 20 minutes

Cooking: 8 hours

Ready In: 8 hours 20 minutes

"A soup that's hearty and tasty. Easy to make! Serve with a crusty whole wheat bread."

INGREDIENTS

1 large, meaty ham hock

4 slices bacon, diced

3 onions, chopped

3 carrots, diced

1 small head cabbage, shredded

3 tablespoons chili powder

1 clove garlic, minced

1 (8 ounce) package 15 bean mixture, soaked overnight

1 (28 ounce) can crushed tomatoes

1 teaspoon chopped fresh sage

salt and pepper to taste

DIRECTIONS

1. Place the ham hock in a 5 to 6 quart slow cooker, and fill half way full with water. Set to High.

2. Heat a large skillet over medium heat. Cook the bacon for a few minutes, then add onions, carrots, and cabbage. Cook, stirring frequently for about 5 minutes. Stir in chili powder and garlic; cook for 2 more minutes. Transfer the mixture to the slow cooker, and add beans, tomatoes, and sage.

3. Cover, and cook 2 hours on High. Reduce heat to Low, and cook for 6 to 7 hours, or until beans are tender. Transfer ham hock to a cutting board, remove meat from bone, and return meat to slow cooker. Season with salt and fresh ground pepper to taste.

Ham Bone Soup

Submitted by: **Charlene Jones**

Makes: 4 servings

Preparation: 30 minutes

Cooking: 6 hours

Ready In: 6 hours 30 minutes

"Homemade soup made easy."

INGREDIENTS

1 ham bone with some meat

1 onion, diced

1 (14.5 ounce) can peeled and diced tomatoes with juice

1 (15.25 ounce) can kidney beans

3 potatoes, cubed

1 green bell pepper, seeded and cubed

4 cups water

6 cubes chicken bouillon

DIRECTIONS

1. Place the ham bone, onion, tomatoes, kidney beans, potatoes, and green pepper into a 3 quart or larger slow cooker. Dissolve the bouillon cubes in water, and pour into the slow cooker.

2. Cover, and cook on High until warm. Reduce heat to Low, and continue to cook for 5 to 6 hours.

Slow Cooker Creamy Potato Soup

Submitted by: **Shirley**

Makes: 6 servings

Preparation: 30 minutes

Cooking: 6 hours 30 minutes

Ready In: 7 hours

"This is a very rich and creamy soup. A great family favorite. It may be cooked on the stove or in a slow cooker. Garnish with chives, if desired."

INGREDIENTS

6 slices bacon, cut into ½ inch pieces

1 onion, finely chopped

2 (10.5 ounce) cans condensed chicken broth

2 cups water

5 large potatoes, diced

½ teaspoon salt

½ teaspoon dried dill weed

½ teaspoon ground white pepper

½ cup all-purpose flour

2 cups half-and-half cream

1 (12 fluid ounce) can evaporated milk

DIRECTIONS

1. Place bacon and onion in a large, deep skillet. Cook over medium-high heat until bacon is evenly brown and onions are soft. Drain off excess grease.

2. Transfer the bacon and onion to a slow cooker, and stir in chicken broth, water, potatoes, salt, dill weed, and white pepper. Cover, and cook on Low 6 to 7 hours, stirring occasionally.

3. In a small bowl, whisk together the flour and half-and-half. Stir into the soup along with the evaporated milk. Cover, and cook another 30 minutes before serving.

Ziti with Italian Sausage

Submitted by: **George Couch**

Makes: 8 servings

Preparation: 15 minutes

Cooking: 1 hour 15 minutes

Ready In: 1 hour 30 minutes

"This recipe is a complete meal. Just add a loaf of fresh bread and you're ready."

INGREDIENTS

1 pound Italian sausage, casings removed

1/2 cup diced celery

1/2 cup diced onion

1 (14.5 ounce) can peeled and diced tomatoes

1 (15 ounce) can tomato sauce

1/4 teaspoon garlic powder

1 1/2 teaspoons salt

1 teaspoon dried oregano

1 pound dry ziti pasta

2 (4.5 ounce) cans sliced mushrooms, drained

8 ounces shredded mozzarella cheese

1/4 cup grated Parmesan cheese

DIRECTIONS

1. In a skillet over medium heat, cook sausage with celery and onion until sausage is evenly browned, about 5 to 10 minutes. Drain excess grease, and set aside.

2. In another skillet over medium-low heat, combine tomatoes, tomato sauce, garlic powder, salt, and oregano. Simmer while preparing pasta.

3. Bring a large pot of lightly salted water to a boil. Cook pasta for 8 to 10 minutes, or until al dente; drain.

4. Preheat oven to 350°F (175°C). In a 3 quart baking dish, layer ziti, mushrooms, sausage, mozzarella cheese, and sauce. Repeat layers, and top with grated Parmesan.

5. Bake for 45 minutes in the preheated oven, or until browned and bubbly.

Cheesy Sausage Zucchini Casserole

Submitted by: **Mandy**

Makes: 8 servings

Preparation: 30 minutes

Cooking: 1 hour

Ready In: 1 hour 30 minutes

"My mom would make this recipe with the zucchini and tomatoes that would flourish in our garden. It's my favorite casserole."

INGREDIENTS

½ cup uncooked white rice

1 cup water

1 pound pork sausage

¼ cup chopped onion

1 cup diced fresh tomato

4 cups cubed zucchini squash

2 (4 ounce) cans sliced mushrooms, drained

1 (8 ounce) package processed cheese food, cubed

1 pinch dried oregano

salt and pepper to taste

DIRECTIONS

1. Combine the rice and water in a small saucepan, and bring to a boil. Reduce heat to low, and simmer for about 20 minutes, or until tender. Remove from heat, and set aside.

2. Preheat the oven to 325°F (165°C).

3. Cook sausage and onion in a large skillet over medium heat, stirring until evenly browned. Drain excess grease. Stir in zucchini and tomatoes, and cook until tender. Stir in rice, mushrooms, and cheese. Season with oregano, salt, and pepper. Spread into a 9x13 inch baking dish, or a 2 quart casserole dish.

4. Bake, uncovered, for 1 hour in the preheated oven, or until lightly browned and bubbly.

Hot Sausage Links and Beans Casserole

Submitted by: **Teri Denlinger**

Makes: 6 servings

Preparation: 30 minutes

Cooking: 50 minutes

Ready In: 1 hour 20 minutes

"Potatoes, beans, sausage and cheese...this is definitely 'stick to your ribs' fare. It's savory, spicy and slightly sweet all at the same time!"

INGREDIENTS

1 tablespoon olive oil

2 cloves garlic, minced

1 cup sliced onion

1 teaspoon dried oregano

1 tablespoon chopped fresh parsley

¼ teaspoon salt

½ teaspoon ground black pepper

1 tablespoon olive oil

4 potatoes, peeled and cubed

½ pound spicy pork sausage links, sliced

½ cup packed brown sugar

2 cups baked beans

¼ cup barbecue sauce

1 cup shredded Cheddar cheese

DIRECTIONS

1. Preheat oven to 350°F (175°C).

2. Heat one tablespoon olive oil in a skillet over medium heat. Add the garlic, and cook for 30 seconds. Stir in the onion, oregano, parsley, salt, and pepper. Cook for 1 minute, and remove from heat.

3. Spread 1 tablespoon olive oil over the bottom of an 8x8 inch glass baking dish. Layer the sliced, cooked potatoes in the dish. Top the potatoes with the onion mixture. Arrange sliced sausage over onions. In a small bowl, stir together the brown sugar, baked beans, and barbecue sauce. Pour evenly over the sausage. Top with shredded Cheddar cheese.

4. Bake in preheated oven for 45 minutes. Serve!

Mushroom Sauce Baked Pork Chops

Submitted by: **J Hilgenberg**

Makes: 6 servings

Preparation: 20 minutes

Cooking: 1 hour 15 minutes

Ready In: 1 hour 35 minutes

"The easiest pork chop recipe imaginable, and oh so tasty. My family has passed this recipe down for years."

INGREDIENTS

6 pork chops

1 teaspoon salt

1/4 teaspoon ground black pepper

garlic powder to taste

2 tablespoons butter

2 large onions, finely chopped

1 (10.75 ounce) can condensed cream of mushroom soup

1 1/4 cups milk

4 cups thinly sliced potatoes

DIRECTIONS

1. Preheat oven to 350°F (175°C). Butter a 2 quart baking dish.

2. Rub pork chops with salt, pepper, and garlic powder. Melt butter in a skillet over medium-high heat, add chops, and brown on both sides. Remove from skillet. Place onions in skillet, and cook until browned. Pour in mushroom soup and milk; stir until blended. Remove from heat, and set aside.

3. Arrange sliced potatoes evenly in prepared baking dish. Arrange chops on top of potatoes. Pour soup mixture over chops.

4. Bake, covered, for 30 minutes in the preheated oven. Uncover, and bake 30 minutes more, or until potatoes are tender.

Pork Chop Casserole III

Submitted by: **Tracy Mantell**

Makes: 5 servings

Preparation: 10 minutes

Cooking: 1 hour

Ready In: 1 hour 10 minutes

"Creamy rice and vegetable pork dish, quick to prepare and sure to please. There are an unlimited number of variations on this, and leftover rice can serve as a side dish later in the week!"

INGREDIENTS

1 cup uncooked white rice

1 (1 ounce) package dry onion soup mix

2 (10.75 ounce) cans condensed cream of mushroom soup

2½ cups water

1 green bell pepper, sliced in rings

1 onion, sliced into rings

5 pork chops

DIRECTIONS

1. Preheat oven to 350°F (175°C).

2. Spread rice in the bottom of a 9x13 inch baking dish. Sprinkle contents of dried onion soup mix over rice. Mix mushroom soup with water, and pour over rice. Arrange the bell pepper and onion slices over soup and rice mixture. Place pork chops on top of pepper and onions. Cover the dish with a lid or aluminum foil.

3. Bake for 1 hour in the preheated oven, until pork chops are very tender, and rice is fully cooked.

Pork Chops with Apples, Onions, and Sweet Potatoes

Submitted by: **Ashbeth**

Makes: 4 servings

Preparation: 15 minutes

Cooking: 1 hour

Ready In: 1 hour 15 minutes

"This is so easy, so good, and so versatile! I've used pork chops with and without bones, pork loin, and pork roast. You can sprinkle the brown sugar, salt, and pepper on the different layers or all at the end, as mentioned in the recipe. Play around with the brown sugar and spices to your taste."

INGREDIENTS

4 pork chops

salt and pepper to taste

2 onions, sliced into rings

2 sweet potatoes, sliced

2 apples - peeled, cored, and sliced into rings

3 tablespoons brown sugar

2 teaspoons freshly ground black pepper

1 teaspoon salt

DIRECTIONS

1. Preheat oven to 375°F (190°C).

2. Season pork chops with salt and pepper to taste, and arrange in a medium oven safe skillet. Top pork chops with onions, sweet potatoes, and apples. Sprinkle with brown sugar. Season with 2 teaspoons pepper and 1 teaspoon salt.

3. Cover, and bake 1 hour in the preheated oven, until sweet potatoes are tender and pork chops have reached an internal temperature of 160°F (70°C).

main dish - poultry

The variety of recipes for poultry is endless. Try your hand at an exotic Adobo-flavored chicken, or stick with the classic chicken and dumplings. Who doesn't enjoy dependable chicken and rice? These recipes wouldn't have become the classics they are without being simple to prepare and consistently delicious.

Fragrant Lemon Chicken

Submitted by: **Dawn Ash**

Makes: 6 servings

Preparation: 20 minutes

Cooking: 9 hours

Ready In: 9 hours 20 minutes

"An easy slow cooker chicken recipe that cooks on its own and tastes great - the meat just falls off the bone!"

INGREDIENTS

1 apple - peeled, cored and quartered

1 stalk celery with leaves, chopped

1 (3 pound) whole chicken

salt to taste

ground black pepper to taste

1 onion, chopped

1/2 teaspoon dried rosemary, crushed

1 lemon, zested and juiced

1 cup hot water

DIRECTIONS

1. Rub salt and pepper into the skin of the chicken, and then place apple and celery inside the chicken. Place chicken in slow cooker. Sprinkle chopped onion, rosemary, and lemon juice and zest over chicken. Pour 1 cup hot water into the slow cooker.

2. Cover, and cook on High for 1 hour. Switch to Low, and cook for 6 to 8 hours, basting several times.

Slow Cooker Lemon Garlic Chicken II

Submitted by: **Carla Joy**

Makes: 6 servings

Preparation: 15 minutes

Cooking: 3 hours 15 minutes

Ready In: 3 hours 30 minutes

"Seasoned, browned chicken breasts slow cooked with lemon juice, garlic, and chicken bouillon. A wonderful 'fix and forget' recipe that is easy and pleases just about everyone. Great served with rice or pasta, or even alone."

INGREDIENTS

1 teaspoon dried oregano

1/2 teaspoon salt

1/4 teaspoon ground black pepper

2 pounds skinless, boneless chicken breast halves

2 tablespoons butter

1/4 cup water

3 tablespoons fresh lemon juice

2 cloves garlic, minced

1 teaspoon chicken bouillon granules

1 teaspoon chopped fresh parsley

DIRECTIONS

1. In a bowl, mix the oregano, salt, and pepper. Rub the mixture into chicken. Melt the butter in a skillet over medium heat. Brown chicken in butter for 3 to 5 minutes on each side. Place chicken in a slow cooker.

2. In the same skillet, mix the water, lemon juice, garlic, and bouillon. Bring the mixture to boil. Pour over the chicken in the slow cooker.

3. Cover, and cook on High for 3 hours, or Low for 6 hours. Add the parsley to the slow cooker 15 to 30 minutes before the end of the cook time.

Baked Slow Cooker Chicken

Submitted by: **'Cotton' Couch**

Makes: 6 servings

Preparation: 20 minutes

Cooking: 10 hours

Ready In: 10 hours 20 minutes

"Baked chicken in a slow cooker for busy people! Put the chicken on in the morning, and have golden brown baked chicken for dinner."

INGREDIENTS

1 (2 to 3 pound) whole chicken

salt and pepper to taste

1 teaspoon paprika

DIRECTIONS

1. Wad three pieces of aluminum foil into 3 to 4 inch balls, and place them in the bottom of the slow cooker.

2. Rinse the chicken, inside and out, under cold running water. Pat dry with paper towels. Season the chicken with the salt, pepper and paprika, and place in the slow cooker on top of the crumbled aluminum foil.

3. Set the slow cooker to High for 1 hour, then turn down to Low for about 8 to 10 hours, or until the chicken is no longer pink and the juices run clear.

Super Easy Slow Cooker Chicken

Submitted by: **Jamie Stringer**

Makes: 4 servings

Preparation: 15 minutes

Cooking: 3 hours

Ready In: 3 hours 15 minutes

"This is super easy and very tasty. You can make more or less; I usually feed my family of 4. My husband who doesn't like chicken says he would eat this every night without complaint."

INGREDIENTS

1 (10.75 ounce) can condensed low fat cream of chicken and herbs soup

1 (4 ounce) can mushroom pieces, drained

½ red onion, chopped

1½ pounds skinless, boneless chicken breast halves - cut into strips

1 dash Marsala wine

DIRECTIONS

1. Combine soup, mushroom pieces, onion, chicken, and wine in slow cooker.

2. Cook on Low setting for 2½ to 3 hours.

Slow Cooker Chicken Parisienne

Submitted by: **Judith Jacobsen**

Makes: 4 to 6 servings

Preparation: 10 minutes

Cooking: 8 hours

Ready In: 8 hours 10 minutes

"Chicken breasts slow cooked with a creamy white wine and mushroom mixture. This quick and easy recipe calls for just five main ingredients, yet is tasty enough to serve for company! My husband normally doesn't like chicken, yet asks for seconds whenever I prepare this. I spoon the sauce over the chicken and serve with rice or noodles."

INGREDIENTS

6 skinless, boneless chicken breast halves

salt and pepper to taste

paprika to taste

1/2 cup dry white wine

1 (10.75 ounce) can condensed cream of mushroom soup

1 (4.5 ounce) can sliced mushrooms, drained

1 cup sour cream

1/4 cup all-purpose flour

DIRECTIONS

1. Sprinkle chicken breasts lightly with salt, pepper, and paprika to taste. Place in slow cooker.

2. In a mixing bowl, combine the wine, condensed soup, and mushrooms. In another bowl, mix together sour cream and flour. Stir sour cream mixture into the mushrooms and wine. Pour over chicken in slow cooker. Sprinkle with additional paprika, if desired.

3. Cover, and cook on Low for 6 to 8 hours.

Slow Cooker Chicken with Mushroom Wine Sauce

Submitted by: **K**

"This is a creamy, tender and very tasty chicken dish. Cooking it in the slow cooker makes it so easy!"

INGREDIENTS

1 (10.75 ounce) can condensed cream of mushroom soup

1 teaspoon dried minced onion

1 teaspoon dried parsley

¼ cup white wine

¼ teaspoon garlic powder

1 tablespoon milk

1 (4 ounce) can mushroom pieces, drained

salt and pepper to taste

4 boneless, skinless chicken breast halves

DIRECTIONS

1. In a slow cooker, mix together the soup, onion, parsley, wine, garlic powder, milk, and mushroom pieces. Season with salt and pepper. Place chicken in the slow cooker, covering with the soup mixture.

2. Cook on Low setting for 5 to 6 hours, or on High setting for 3 to 4 hours.

No Time to Cook Chicken

Submitted by: **Sue Ann Buck**

Makes: 4 servings

Preparation: 10 minutes

Cooking: 8 hours

Ready In: 8 hours 10 minutes

"Chicken, creamy soups, and sour cream in a slow cooker - cook all day, ready for you when you get home. Only 4 ingredients! Everyone loves this, a no hassle dinner good enough for company."

INGREDIENTS

4 skinless, boneless chicken breast halves

1 (10.75 ounce) can condensed cream of chicken soup

1 (10.75 ounce) can condensed cream of celery soup

½ cup sour cream

DIRECTIONS

1. Place chicken breasts in a slow cooker. In a medium bowl, mix the cream of chicken soup and cream of celery soup until smooth Pour over the chicken, making sure it is well coated.

2. Cover, and cook on Low heat for 7 to 8 hours. Stir in the sour cream about ½ hour before serving.

Easy and Delicious Chicken

Submitted by: **Monika Polly**

Makes: 6 servings

Preparation: 15 minutes

Cooking: 9 hours

Ready In: 9 hours 15 minutes

"A slow cooker recipe that is the best! You can start with frozen chicken breasts without having to adjust the cooking time."

INGREDIENTS

6 skinless, boneless chicken breast halves

1 (8 ounce) bottle Italian-style salad dressing

1 (10.75 ounce) can condensed cream of chicken soup

1 cup chicken broth

1 (8 ounce) package cream cheese

1/2 teaspoon dried basil

1/2 teaspoon dried thyme

salt and pepper to taste

DIRECTIONS

1. In a slow cooker, combine the chicken breasts and Italian-style dressing.

2. Cover, and cook on Low for 6 to 8 hours.

3. Drain off the juices, and shred the chicken meat. In a medium bowl, mix the soup, broth, cream cheese, basil, thyme, salt, and pepper. Pour over the chicken in the slow cooker. Continue cooking on Low for 1 hour.

Slow Cooker Tipsy Chicken

Submitted by: **Foxworth**

Makes: 8 servings

Preparation: 15 minutes

Cooking: 8 hours

Ready In: 8 hours 15 minutes

"Chicken thighs simmered in creamy soups with olives, mushrooms, and white wine. A let-it-cook-all-day dish with wonderful flavor. Serve over hot cooked rice."

INGREDIENTS

1 tablespoon butter

8 chicken thighs

salt and pepper to taste

1 (10.75 ounce) can condensed cream of celery soup

1 (10.75 ounce) can condensed cream of mushroom soup

1 (5 ounce) jar pimento-stuffed green olives

1 (8 ounce) package sliced fresh mushrooms

1¼ cups Chablis wine

1 tablespoon all-purpose flour

DIRECTIONS

1. Melt the butter in a large skillet over medium-high heat. Season the chicken with salt and pepper, and brown for 2 to 3 minutes each side. Place in a slow cooker.

2. In a saucepan over medium heat, blend the cream of mushroom soup and cream of celery soup. Pour over the chicken in the slow cooker, then add olives, mushrooms, wine, and flour.

3. Cover, and cook on Low for 8 hours.

Slow Cooker Adobo Chicken

Submitted by: **Adrienne Lapp**

Makes: 4 servings

Preparation: 30 minutes

Cooking: 8 hours

Ready In: 8 hours 30 minutes

"An easy slow cooker recipe for a whole chicken. This is such a simple recipe for something SO good! Serve hot with steamed rice."

INGREDIENTS

1 small sweet onion, sliced

8 cloves garlic, crushed

¾ cup soy sauce

½ cup vinegar

1 (3 pound) whole chicken, cut into pieces

DIRECTIONS

1. Place chicken in a slow cooker. In a small bowl mix the onion, garlic, soy sauce, and vinegar, and pour over the chicken. Cook on Low for 6 to 8 hours.

Slow Cooker Sweet and Tangy Chicken

Submitted by: **Jan**

Makes: 8 servings

Preparation: 10 minutes

Cooking: 9 hours

Ready In: 9 hours 10 minutes

"Very, very good! Serve the chicken and sauce over rice."

INGREDIENTS

2 (18 ounce) bottles barbeque sauce

1 (15 ounce) can pineapple chunks

1 green bell pepper, chopped

1 onion, chopped

2 cloves garlic, minced

8 boneless, skinless chicken breast halves

DIRECTIONS

1. In a large bowl, mix together barbecue sauce, pineapple with juice, green bell pepper, onion, and garlic.

2. Arrange 4 of the chicken breasts in the bottom of a slow cooker. Pour half or the barbecue sauce over the chicken. Place remaining chicken in slow cooker, and pour remaining sauce over the top.

3. Cover, and cook on Low for 8 to 9 hours.

Slow Cooker Chicken Creole

Submitted by: **Mary Moon**

Makes: 4 servings

Preparation: 10 minutes

Cooking: 12 hours

Ready In: 12 hours 10 minutes

"The stewed tomatoes and jalapeno pepper give this slow cooker recipe its Creole zing, along with seasoning and other veggies. This is an easy and tasty Creole chicken recipe. Just put all ingredients into the slow cooker and let it simmer all day. It's perfect over egg noodles. Add extra water and veggies to the leftovers to make a tasty afternoon soup."

INGREDIENTS

4 skinless, boneless chicken breast halves

salt and pepper to taste

Creole-style seasoning to taste

1 (14.5 ounce) can stewed tomatoes, with liquid

1 stalk celery, diced

1 green bell pepper, diced

3 cloves garlic, minced

1 onion, diced

1 (4 ounce) can mushrooms, drained

1 fresh jalapeno pepper, seeded and chopped

DIRECTIONS

1. Place chicken breasts in slow cooker. Season with salt, pepper, and Creole-style seasoning to taste. Stir in tomatoes with liquid, celery, bell pepper, garlic, onion, mushrooms, and jalapeno pepper.

2. Cook on Low for 10 to 12 hours, or on High for 5 to 6 hours.

Creole Chicken

Submitted by: **Nancy**

Makes: 8 servings

Preparation: 15 minutes

Cooking: 5 hours 20 minutes

Ready In: 5 hours 35 minutes

"This is a family favorite and easy to prepare in the slow cooker. The chicken has a bite to it but one can control the heat by limiting the amount of hot pepper sauce used. Even if you don't like very hot food, include a few drops for flavor. (For the ham, I get the deli to slice about a one inch section of Virginia Ham)."

INGREDIENTS

8 chicken thighs

¼ pound cooked ham, cut into one inch cubes

1 (16 ounce) can diced tomatoes

1 green bell pepper, chopped

6 green onions, chopped

1 (6 ounce) can tomato paste

1 teaspoon salt

2 dashes hot pepper sauce

2 cups water

1 cup uncooked long grain white rice

½ pound Polish sausage, sliced diagonally

DIRECTIONS

1. In a slow cooker, place the chicken, ham, tomatoes, bell pepper, green onions, tomato paste, salt, and hot pepper sauce. Cover, and cook on Low for 4 to 5 hours.

2. Combine water and rice in a medium saucepan. Bring to a boil. Reduce heat, cover, and simmer for 20 minutes.

3. Mix the cooked rice and sausage into the slow cooker. Cover, and cook on High for 15 to 20 minutes, or until the sausage is heated through.

Slow Cooker Chicken Cacciatore

Submitted by: **Rosie**

Makes: 6 servings

Preparation: 15 minutes

Cooking: 9 hours

Ready In: 9 hours 15 minutes

"Easy slow cooker chicken cacciatore. Serve over angel hair pasta. 'Cacciatore' is Italian for 'hunter', and this American-Italian term refers to food prepared 'hunter style,' with mushrooms and onions. Avanti!"

INGREDIENTS

6 skinless, boneless chicken breast halves

1 (28 ounce) jar spaghetti sauce

2 green bell pepper, seeded and cubed

8 ounces fresh mushrooms, sliced

1 onion, finely diced

2 tablespoons minced garlic

DIRECTIONS

1. Put the chicken in the slow cooker. Top with the spaghetti sauce, green bell peppers, mushrooms, onion, and garlic.

2. Cover, and cook on Low for 7 to 9 hours.

Slow Cooker Chicken and Dumplings

Submitted by: **Janiece Mason**

Makes: 8 servings

Preparation: 10 minutes

Cooking: 6 hours

Ready In: 6 hours 10 minutes

"This is an easy slow cooker recipe that cooks while you are at work! It is wonderful on a cold, snowy day. I have four children who are picky eaters, and they LOVE this! Enjoy!"

INGREDIENTS

4 skinless, boneless chicken breast halves

2 tablespoons butter

2 (10.75 ounce) cans condensed cream of chicken soup

1 onion, finely diced

2 (10 ounce) packages refrigerated biscuit dough, torn into pieces

DIRECTIONS

1. Place the chicken, butter, soup, and onion in a slow cooker, and fill with enough water to cover.

2. Cover, and cook for 5 to 6 hours on High. About 30 minutes before serving, place the torn biscuit dough in the slow cooker. Cook until the dough is no longer raw in the center.

Chicken and Corn Chili

Submitted by: **Sarah Jane**

Makes: 6 servings

Preparation: 15 minutes

Cooking: 12 hours

Ready In: 12 hours 15 minutes

"This is an easy slow cooker meal - use your imagination and season it up as you like! Great on a c-c-c-cold winter night! I serve this with grated cheese, sour cream, chopped cilantro and green onions, and flour tortillas on the side."

INGREDIENTS

4 skinless, boneless chicken breast halves

1 (16 ounce) jar salsa

2 teaspoons garlic powder

1 teaspoon ground cumin

1 teaspoon chili powder

salt to taste

ground black pepper to taste

1 (11 ounce) can Mexican-style corn

1 (15 ounce) can pinto beans

DIRECTIONS

1. Place chicken and salsa in the slow cooker the night before you want to eat this chili. Season with garlic powder, cumin, chili powder, salt, and pepper. Cook 6 to 8 hours on Low setting.

2. About 3 to 4 hours before you want to eat, shred the chicken with 2 forks. Return the meat to the pot, and continue cooking.

3. Stir the corn and the pinto beans into the slow cooker. Simmer until ready to serve.

Momma OB's Chicken Chili

Submitted by: **Betty O'Brien**

Makes: 8 servings

Preparation: 15 minutes

Cooking: 3 hours

Ready In: 3 hours 15 minutes

"This is my version of Chicken Chili, it was kinda thrown together for work and EVERYONE loved it."

INGREDIENTS

2 pounds skinless, boneless chicken breast meat - cubed

½ tablespoon olive oil

1 tablespoon Italian seasoning

2 (28 ounce) cans whole peeled tomatoes

1 (16 ounce) can chili beans, drained and rinsed

1 (15 ounce) can kidney beans, drained and rinsed

1 (1.25 ounce) package chili seasoning mix

1 (4 ounce) can diced green chile peppers

1 onion, minced

3 cloves garlic, minced

½ cup water

DIRECTIONS

1. Heat oil in a skillet over medium heat, and add the chicken and half of the Italian seasoning. Cook, stirring frequently, until chicken is cooked through and evenly browned.

2. Place the remaining Italian seasoning, tomatoes, chili beans, kidney beans, chili seasoning, chile peppers, onion, garlic, and water in a slow cooker. Stir in chicken and juices

3. Cover, and cook on High for three hours.

Chicken Broth in a Slow Cooker

Submitted by: **Micki Stout**

Makes: 5 servings

Preparation: 15 minutes

Cooking: 10 hours

Ready In: 10 hours 15 minutes

"This is the recipe I use to make chicken broth for use in other recipes. Because it's done in the slow cooker, you don't need to fuss with it. I like to use breasts and wings, but any bone in pieces will make a nice broth."

INGREDIENTS

2½ pounds bone-in chicken pieces

6 cups water

2 stalks celery, chopped

2 carrots, chopped

1 onion, quartered

1 tablespoon dried basil

DIRECTIONS

1. Place the chicken pieces, celery, carrots, onion, and basil in a slow cooker.

2. Cook on Low setting for 8 to 10 hours. Strain before using, and discard vegetables. Chicken may be removed from the bones, and used in soup.

Chicken and Spinach Alfredo Lasagna

Submitted by: **Sue**

Makes: 12 servings

Preparation: 30 minutes

Cooking: 1 hour 30 minutes

Ready In: 2 hours

"A different, yet wonderful twist on normal lasagna!"

INGREDIENTS

1 (8 ounce) package lasagna noodles

3 cups heavy cream

2 (10.75 ounce) cans condensed cream of mushroom soup

1 cup grated Parmesan cheese

¼ cup butter

1 tablespoon olive oil

½ large onion, diced

4 cloves garlic, sliced

5 mushrooms, diced

1 roasted chicken, shredded

salt and ground black pepper to taste

1 cup ricotta cheese

1 bunch fresh spinach, rinsed

3 cups shredded mozzarella cheese

DIRECTIONS

1. Preheat oven to 350°F (175°C). Bring a large pot of lightly salted water to a boil. Cook lasagna noodles for 8 to 10 minutes, or until al dente. Drain, and rinse with cold water.

2. In a saucepan over low heat, mix together heavy cream, cream of mushroom soup, Parmesan cheese, and butter. Simmer, stirring frequently, until well blended.

3. Heat the olive oil in a skillet over medium heat. Cook and stir the onion in olive oil until tender, then add garlic and mushrooms. Mix in the chicken, and cook until heated through. Season with salt and pepper.

4. Lightly coat the bottom of a 9x13 inch baking dish with enough of the cream sauce mixture to coat. Layer with ⅓ of the lasagna noodles, ½ cup ricotta, ½ of the spinach, ½ the chicken mixture, and 1 cup mozzarella. Top with ½ the cream sauce mixture, and repeat the layers. Place the remaining noodles on top, and spread with remaining sauce.

5. Bake 1 hour in the preheated oven, or until brown and bubbly. Top with the remaining mozzarella, and continue baking until cheese is melted and lightly browned.

White Cheese Chicken Lasagna

Submitted by: Lisa Humpf

Makes: 12 servings

Preparation: 25 minutes

Cooking: 50 minutes

Ready In: 1 hour 15 minutes

"A chicken and spinach lasagna with a creamy white cheese sauce. Great for any kind of pot luck. My kids love it."

INGREDIENTS

9 lasagna noodles

½ cup butter

1 onion, chopped

1 clove garlic, minced

½ cup all-purpose flour

1 teaspoon salt

2 cups chicken broth

1½ cups milk

4 cups shredded mozzarella cheese, divided

1 cup grated Parmesan cheese

1 teaspoon dried basil

1 teaspoon dried oregano

½ teaspoon ground black pepper

2 cups ricotta cheese

2 cups cubed, cooked chicken meat

2 (10 ounce) packages frozen chopped spinach, thawed and drained

1 tablespoon chopped fresh parsley

¼ cup grated Parmesan cheese for topping

DIRECTIONS

1. Preheat oven to 350°F (175°C). Bring a large pot of lightly salted water to a boil. Cook lasagna noodles in boiling water for 8 to 10 minutes. Drain, and rinse with cold water.

2. Melt the butter in a large saucepan over medium heat. Cook the onion and garlic in the butter until tender, stirring frequently. Stir in the flour and salt, and simmer until bubbly. Mix in the broth and milk, and boil, stirring constantly, for 1 minute. Stir in 2 cups mozzarella cheese and ½ cup Parmesan cheese. Season with the basil, oregano, and ground black pepper. Remove from heat, and set aside.

3. Spread ⅓ of the sauce mixture in the bottom of a 9x13 inch baking dish. Layer with ⅓ of the noodles, the ricotta, and the chicken. Arrange ⅓ of the noodles over the chicken, and layer with ⅓ of the sauce mixture, spinach, and the remaining 2 cups mozzarella cheese and ½ cup Parmesan cheese. Arrange remaining noodles over cheese, and spread remaining sauce evenly over noodles. Sprinkle with parsley and ¼ cup Parmesan cheese.

4. Bake 35 to 40 minutes in the preheated oven.

Creamy Chicken Lasagna

Submitted by: **Caroline**

Makes: 6 servings

Preparation: 25 minutes

Cooking: 1 hour 5 minutes

Ready In: 1 hour 30 minutes

"This is an unusual but fantastic combination. Everyone that tastes it raves!"

INGREDIENTS

3 skinless, boneless chicken breast halves

6 uncooked lasagna noodles

1 cube chicken bouillon

¼ cup hot water

1 (8 ounce) package cream cheese, softened

2 cups shredded mozzarella cheese

1 (26 ounce) jar spaghetti sauce

DIRECTIONS

1. Bring a large pot of lightly salted water to a boil. Cook lasagna noodles for 8 to 10 minutes, or until al dente. Drain, rinse with cold water, and set aside.

2. Meanwhile, place the chicken in a saucepan with enough water to cover, and bring to a boil. Cook for 20 minutes, or until no longer pink and juices run clear. Remove from saucepan, and shred.

3. Preheat oven to 350°F (175°C). Dissolve the bouillon cube in hot water. In a large bowl, mix the chicken with the bouillon, cream cheese, and 1 cup mozzarella cheese.

4. Spread ⅓ of spaghetti sauce in the bottom of a 9 inch square baking dish. Cover with the chicken mixture, and top with 3 lasagna noodles; repeat. Top with remaining sauce, and sprinkle with remaining mozzarella cheese.

5. Bake for 45 minutes in the preheated oven.

Fresh Asparagus and Chicken Casserole

Submitted by: **Kathy Sauers**

Makes: 6 servings

Preparation: 30 minutes

Cooking: 45 minutes

Ready In: 1 hour 15 minutes

"Great in the spring when asparagus first comes in and you can get it fresh."

INGREDIENTS

1 (8 ounce) package egg noodles

1⅓ tablespoons olive oil

1 onion, chopped

1 cup chopped, cooked chicken meat

1 red bell pepper, chopped

2 stalks celery, chopped

1 cup chicken stock

1½ cups sour cream

½ teaspoon dried oregano

1 pound fresh asparagus, trimmed and cut into 2 inch pieces

8 tablespoons grated Parmesan cheese, divided

DIRECTIONS

1. Preheat oven to 350°F (175°C). Lightly grease a 1½ quart casserole dish.

2. Cook noodles in a large pot of boiling water for 5 minutes, or until almost tender. Drain, and rinse under cold water.

3. Heat the olive oil in a heavy skillet over medium heat. Cook onion for 4 to 5 minutes, stirring frequently. Add chicken, red bell pepper, celery, and chicken stock. Bring to a boil, and simmer for 5 minutes. Stir in sour cream and oregano.

4. Spread half of the chicken mixture into the prepared dish. Arrange asparagus over chicken, spread cooked noodles evenly over asparagus, and top with the remaining chicken mixture. Sprinkle with Parmesan cheese.

5. Bake 30 minutes in the preheated oven, until lightly brown.

Wanda's Chicken Noodle Bake

Submitted by: **Cindy**

Makes: 6 to 8 servings

Preparation: 15 minutes

Cooking: 45 minutes

Ready In: 1 hour

"An egg noodle/chicken casserole with celery, onion, carrots, mushrooms and a creamy cheese sauce. This was brought to us by one of our kind church ladies after the birth of son number 3! I begged her for the recipe...and now Wanda passes it on to all of you."

INGREDIENTS

1²/₃ cups uncooked egg noodles

3 tablespoons butter

1 stalk celery, chopped

¹/₄ cup chopped onion

2 (10.75 ounce) cans condensed cream of chicken soup

2 cups milk

2 cups shredded Cheddar cheese

1 (16 ounce) can diced carrots, drained

1 (4.5 ounce) can sliced mushrooms

3 cups cooked, cubed chicken or turkey meat

1 teaspoon salt

¹/₄ teaspoon ground black pepper

¹/₂ cup dry bread crumbs

DIRECTIONS

1. Bring a large pot of water to a boil. Cook noodles in boiling water for about 8 minutes, or until done. Drain.

2. Preheat oven to 350°F (175°C). Coat a 9x13 inch pan with cooking spray.

3. In a saucepan, melt butter over medium heat. Cook celery and onion in butter until tender, stirring frequently. Stir in soup, milk, and cheese. Cook, stirring, until cheese melts.

4. In a large bowl, mix together the noodles, cheese sauce mixture, carrots, mushrooms, chicken, and salt and pepper. Spread mixture evenly into the prepared baking dish. Top with bread crumbs.

5. Bake in preheated oven for 30 minutes, or until hot.

Ham and Chicken Casserole

Submitted by: **Jan Taylor**

Makes: 2 servings

Preparation: 20 minutes

Cooking: 35 minutes

Ready In: 55 minutes

"A creamy casserole with chicken, ham, noodles, and celery. Perfect for using that leftover Easter ham or other dinner leftovers in a quick, tasty family dish."

INGREDIENTS

½ cup uncooked egg noodles

2 tablespoons butter

2 tablespoons all-purpose flour

1 cup milk

½ cup cooked, cubed chicken breast meat

½ cup cooked, diced ham

¼ cup chopped celery

¼ teaspoon salt

¼ teaspoon ground black pepper

3 ounces shredded Cheddar cheese

1 teaspoon paprika

DIRECTIONS

1. Preheat oven to 400°F (200°C). Lightly grease a medium baking dish.

2. Bring a saucepan of lightly salted water to a boil. Cook egg noodles in boiling water for 6 to 8 minutes, or until al dente. Drain.

3. Melt butter in a saucepan over medium-low heat. Mix in flour, heating until bubbly. Slowly whisk in milk. Cook for 5 minutes, stirring constantly, or until thick and smooth. Remove the saucepan from heat. Mix in the noodles, chicken, ham, celery, salt, and pepper. Spoon the mixture into the prepared baking dish.

4. Bake for 15 minutes in the preheated oven. Sprinkle with cheese and paprika, and continue baking for another 5 minutes. Serve hot!

Chicken Tetrazzini IV

Submitted by: **Mary**

Makes: 4 servings

Preparation: 15 minutes

Cooking: 45 minutes

Ready In: 1 hour

"Chicken, mushrooms and spaghetti baked in a rich, creamy white sauce flavored with Parmesan cheese and sherry."

INGREDIENTS

1 (8 ounce) package spaghetti, broken into pieces

¼ cup butter

¼ cup all-purpose flour

¾ teaspoon salt

¼ teaspoon ground black pepper

1 cup chicken broth

1 cup heavy cream

2 tablespoons sherry

1 (4.5 ounce) can sliced mushrooms, drained

2 cups chopped cooked chicken

½ cup grated Parmesan cheese

DIRECTIONS

1. Preheat oven to 350°F (175°C). Lightly grease a 9x13 inch baking dish.

2. Bring a large pot of lightly salted water to a boil. Add spaghetti, and cook for 8 to 10 minutes, or until al dente; drain.

3. Meanwhile, in a large saucepan, melt butter over low heat. Stir in flour, salt, and pepper. Cook, stirring, until smooth. Remove from heat, and gradually stir in chicken broth and cream.

4. Return to heat, and bring to a low boil for 1 minute, stirring constantly. Add sherry, then stir in cooked spaghetti, mushrooms, and chicken. Pour mixture into the prepared baking dish, and top with Parmesan cheese.

5. Bake 30 minutes in the preheated oven, until bubbly and lightly browned.

Almond Chicken Casserole

Submitted by: **Behr Kleine**

Makes: 12 servings

Preparation: 15 minutes

Cooking: 1 hour 5 minutes

Ready In: 1 hour 20 minutes

"This dish refrigerates and freezes well, so it can be prepared ahead and stored."

INGREDIENTS

1½ cups uncooked long grain white rice

3 cups water

5 cups diced cooked chicken

½ cup mayonnaise

½ cup plain yogurt

1 (10.75 ounce) can condensed cream of mushroom soup

2 cups chicken broth

2 tablespoons lemon juice

3 tablespoons chopped onion

1 (8 ounce) can water chestnuts

1½ cups sliced almonds

1 cup chopped celery

2 teaspoons ground white pepper

1 tablespoon salt

3 cups cornflakes cereal

1 cup butter, melted

DIRECTIONS

1. Combine rice and water in a saucepan, and bring to a boil. Reduce heat, cover, and simmer for 20 minutes.

2. Preheat oven to 350°F (175°C). Lightly grease a 9x13 inch baking dish.

3. In a large bowl stir together the cooked rice, diced chicken, mayonnaise, yogurt, cream of mushroom soup, and chicken broth. Mix in the lemon juice, onion, water chestnuts, 1 cup of sliced almonds, and celery. Season with white pepper and salt. Transfer the mixture to the prepared baking dish.

4. In a bowl, toss the remaining ½ cup sliced almonds and cornflakes cereal with the melted butter. Spread evenly over the casserole.

5. Bake 35 to 45 minutes in the preheated oven, until lightly browned.

Creamy Chicken Asparagus Casserole

Submitted by: **Kathy Sauers**

Makes: 4 servings

Preparation: 25 minutes

Cooking: 35 minutes

Ready In: 1 hour

"A nice one dish casserole. Tender asparagus and tarragon add a delicate note to this almond-topped delight!"

INGREDIENTS

1 teaspoon unsalted butter

4 skinless, boneless chicken breast halves

1 onion, finely diced

1 pound fresh asparagus, trimmed and cut into 2½ inch pieces

1 teaspoon dried tarragon

1½ cups cream of chicken soup

¼ cup sliced almonds

1⅓ cups water

⅔ cup uncooked long grain white rice

DIRECTIONS

1. Preheat oven to 375°F (190°C).

2. Melt the butter in an ovenproof skillet over medium-high heat, and brown the chicken breasts about 3 minutes on each side. Remove chicken from the skillet, and set aside. Add the onions and asparagus to the skillet; cook for 4 to 5 minutes, or until the onions are tender. Arrange the chicken breasts over the onions and asparagus, and season with tarragon. Pour soup over chicken.

3. Cover the skillet, and bake for 15 minutes in the preheated oven. Remove cover, sprinkle with almonds, and bake for another 5 minutes.

4. Meanwhile, combine water and rice in a saucepan. Bring to a boil. Reduce heat, cover, and simmer for 20 minutes. Serve chicken and asparagus over rice.

The Best Artichoke Chicken Buffet

Submitted by: **Eden**

Makes: 16 servings

Preparation: 20 minutes

Cooking: 2 hours

Ready In: 2 hours 20 minutes

"Wild rice and chicken pieces mixed with a plethora of vegetables, sherry and cream and baked into a delectable 'buffet'!"

INGREDIENTS

10 thick slices bacon

1²/₃ cups uncooked wild rice

5 cups water

1 cup butter

1 small onion, chopped

10 fresh mushrooms, sliced

2 (10.75 ounce) cans condensed cream of chicken soup

¹/₂ cup heavy cream

¹/₂ cup sherry

1 teaspoon salt

3 cups cooked, cubed chicken breast meat

2 (14 ounce) cans artichoke hearts, drained

2 cups julienned carrots

3 cups shredded mozzarella cheese

¹/₄ cup grated Parmesan cheese

DIRECTIONS

1. Combine wild rice and water in a saucepan, and bring to a boil. Reduce heat, cover, and simmer for 40 to 50 minutes.

2. Place bacon in a large, deep skillet. Cook over medium-high heat until evenly browned. Drain, crumble, and set aside.

3. In a large saucepan, melt butter over medium heat. Cook onion and mushrooms in butter until soft. Stir in soup, cream, sherry, and salt; cook until hot.

4. Preheat oven to 350°F (175°C), and lightly grease a 9x13 inch baking dish. In a large bowl, mix together cooked bacon, soup mixture, chicken meat, artichoke hearts, carrots, and mozzarella cheese. Spread cooked rice in the bottom of the baking dish, then spread chicken and artichoke mixture over rice. Top with Parmesan cheese.

5. Cover, and bake in preheated oven for 30 minutes. Remove cover, and bake for an additional 30 minutes.

Chicken Spectacular

Submitted by: **Jodi D**

Makes: 10 servings

Preparation: 15 minutes

Cooking: 1 hour 20 minutes

Ready In: 1 hour 35 minutes

"A very good casserole that makes a lot. This dish also freezes well, so it's great to make ahead and warm up later!"

INGREDIENTS

3 cups water

1 cup uncooked wild rice

3 cups cooked, cubed chicken breast meat

1 (10.75 ounce) can condensed cream of celery soup

1 (4 ounce) jar diced pimento peppers, drained

1 onion, chopped

2 (14.5 ounce) cans French-style green beans, drained

1 cup mayonnaise

1 cup water chestnuts, drained and chopped

salt and pepper to taste

DIRECTIONS

1. Combine water and wild rice in a saucepan, and bring to a boil. Reduce heat, cover, and simmer for 50 minutes, or until tender.

2. Preheat oven to 350°F (175°C).

3. In a large bowl, toss together the cooked rice, chicken, cream of celery soup, pimentos, onion, green beans, mayonnaise, water chestnuts, salt, and pepper. Transfer to a 3 quart casserole dish.

4. Bake in the preheated oven for 25 to 30 minutes, or until heated through.

Poppy Seed Poultry Casserole

Submitted by: **Dierdre Dee**

Makes: 8 servings

Preparation: 15 minutes

Cooking: 50 minutes

Ready In: 1 hour 10 minutes

"A good way to use leftover chicken or turkey."

INGREDIENTS

2 cups water

1 cup uncooked long grain white rice

1 (10.75 ounce) can condensed cream of chicken soup

1 (8 ounce) container sour cream

1 tablespoon poppy seeds

1 teaspoon dried dill weed

4 cups cooked, cubed chicken meat

1/2 cup butter, melted

1 1/2 cups crushed buttery round crackers

DIRECTIONS

1. Combine water and rice in a saucepan, and bring to a boil. Reduce heat, cover, and simmer for 20 minutes.

2. Preheat oven to 350°F (175°C). Lightly grease a 9x13 inch baking dish.

3. In a large bowl, mix the soup, sour cream, poppy seeds, and dill. Stir in the chicken and cooked rice. Spread the mixture into the prepared baking dish. In a small bowl, mix the cracker crumbs and butter; sprinkle over the casserole.

4. Bake in the preheated oven for 30 minutes. Let cool for 5 minutes before serving.

Salsa Chicken Rice Casserole

Submitted by: **Tami**

Makes: 8 servings

Preparation: 20 minutes

Cooking: 1 hour

Ready In: 1 hour 20 minutes

"Layers of rice, chicken breast, a creamy soup and salsa mixture and two kinds of cheese add up to a simply yummy salsa casserole! This recipe is a family favorite because it's delicious and easily made with ingredients found in the pantry."

INGREDIENTS

1¹⁄₃ cups uncooked white rice

2²⁄₃ cups water

4 skinless, boneless chicken breast halves

2 cups shredded Monterey Jack cheese

2 cups shredded Cheddar cheese

1 (10.75 ounce) can condensed cream of chicken soup

1 (10.75 ounce) can condensed cream of mushroom soup

1 onion, chopped

1¹⁄₂ cups mild salsa

4 cups cooked white rice

DIRECTIONS

1. Place rice and water in a saucepan, and bring to a boil. Reduce heat to low, cover, and simmer for 20 minutes.

2. Meanwhile, place chicken breast halves into a large saucepan, and fill the pan with water. Bring to a boil, and cook for 20 minutes, or until done. Remove chicken from water. When cool enough to handle, cut meat into bite-size pieces.

3. Preheat oven to 350°F (175°C). Lightly grease a 9x13 inch baking dish.

4. In a medium bowl, combine Monterey Jack and Cheddar cheeses. In a separate bowl, mix together cream of chicken soup, cream of mushroom soup, onion, and salsa. Layer ½ of the rice, ½ of the chicken, ½ of the soup and salsa mixture, and ½ of the cheese mixture in prepared dish. Repeat layers, ending with cheese.

5. Bake in preheated oven for about 40 minutes, or until bubbly.

Chicken and Wild Rice Casserole

Submitted by: Katherine Denning

Makes: 10 servings

Preparation: 30 minutes

Cooking: 2 hours

Ready In: 2 hours 30 minutes

"A creamy chicken, wild rice, and mushroom casserole. This elegant, tasty recipe may be made in advance and baked right before company arrives! It's a real family favorite! Serve with French-style green beans or broccoli, fruit salad and French bread. That's all you need."

INGREDIENTS

3 pounds bone-in chicken breast halves, with skin

1 cup water

1 cup dry white wine

1½ teaspoons salt

1 teaspoon curry powder

1 onion, sliced

1 cup chopped celery

2 (6 ounce) packages long grain and wild rice mix

1 (16 ounce) can sliced mushrooms, drained

1 cup sour cream

1 (10.75 ounce) can condensed cream of mushroom soup

DIRECTIONS

1. Place chicken breasts in a large pot with water, wine, salt, curry powder, onion, and celery. Cover, and bring to a boil. Reduce heat to low, and simmer for 1 hour. Remove from heat, strain (reserving broth), and refrigerate to cool. Remove chicken meat from bone, and cut into bite size pieces.

2. Prepare the rice mix according to package directions. Replace the specified amount of liquid with the same amount of the reserved broth.

3. Preheat oven to 350°F (175°C). Lightly grease a 9x13 inch baking dish.

4. In a large bowl combine the chicken, rice, and mushrooms. Blend in the sour cream and soup. Spoon into the prepared baking dish.

5. Bake at 350°F (175°C) for 1 hour.

Swiss Chicken Casserole

Submitted by: **Melanie Burton**

Makes: 6 servings

Preparation: 10 minutes

Cooking: 50 minutes

Ready In: 1 hour

"A tasty spin on the usual chicken and stuffing casserole. Great served with rice or egg noodles."

INGREDIENTS

6 skinless, boneless chicken breast halves

6 slices Swiss cheese

1 (10.75 ounce) can condensed cream of chicken soup

¼ cup milk

1 (8 ounce) package dry bread stuffing mix

½ cup melted butter

DIRECTIONS

1. Preheat oven to 350°F (175°C). Lightly grease a 9x13 inch baking dish.

2. Arrange chicken breasts in the baking dish. Place one slice of Swiss cheese on top of each chicken breast. Combine cream of chicken soup and milk in a medium bowl, and pour over chicken breasts. Sprinkle with stuffing mix. Pour melted butter over top, and cover with foil.

3. Bake 50 minutes, or until chicken is no longer pink and juices run clear.

Chicken Supreme III

Submitted by: **Dusti Fees**

Makes: 6 servings

Preparation: 20 minutes

Cooking: 40 minutes

Ready In: 1 hour

"Very easy and quick recipe, and nearly a whole meal by itself!"

INGREDIENTS

4 skinless, boneless chicken breast half - cut into cubes

1 onion, chopped

¾ cup butter, melted

1⅓ cups water

6 ounces dry bread stuffing mix

¼ cup water

1 (10.75 ounce) can condensed cream of chicken soup

1 cup shredded Cheddar cheese

DIRECTIONS

1. In a non-stick skillet over medium heat, cook and stir the chicken and onion until the chicken is no longer pink and juices run clear.

2. Preheat oven to 350°F (175°C). Lightly grease a 2 quart casserole dish.

3. In a medium bowl, blend the melted butter, 1⅓ cups water, and dry stuffing mix. Place ½ the chicken and onion mixture in the prepared dish, and cover with the stuffing mixture. Cover with the remaining chicken mixture. In a small bowl, mix the ¼ cup water and cream of chicken soup, and pour into the dish. Top with the Cheddar cheese.

4. Bake 30 minutes in the preheated oven, or until bubbly and lightly browned.

Thanksgiving Leftover Casserole

Submitted by: **Sharon Pruitt**

Makes: 8 servings

Preparation: 20 minutes

Cooking: 55 minutes

Ready In: 1 hour 15 minutes

"Turkey, mashed potatoes, cheese, a special sauce, and some little extras combine to make a tasty casserole for 'the day after.' Absolutely delicious way to use those tasty Thanksgiving leftovers."

INGREDIENTS

3 tablespoons butter

2 tablespoons all-purpose flour

1 (12 fluid ounce) can evaporated milk

1 cup water

1/4 teaspoon salt

1/4 teaspoon freshly ground black pepper

1/4 teaspoon onion powder

2 tablespoons butter

1 cup finely crushed herb-seasoned dry bread stuffing mix

1 cup cooked, diced turkey meat

1 cup shredded Cheddar cheese

2 cups leftover mashed potatoes

DIRECTIONS

1. Preheat oven to 350°F (175°C). Lightly grease a 9x13 inch baking dish.

2. Melt 3 tablespoons butter in a saucepan over low heat. Blend in the flour. Slowly stir in evaporated milk and water, then season with salt, pepper, and onion powder. Stir sauce over low heat for 5 minutes.

3. In a separate saucepan over low heat, melt 2 tablespoons butter. Blend in the dry stuffing mix. Place the turkey in the prepared baking dish. Pour the sauce over turkey, then sprinkle with Cheddar cheese. Spread mashed potatoes over cheese. Top mashed potatoes with the stuffing mixture.

4. Bake 45 minutes in the preheated oven.

Chicken and Biscuit Casserole

Submitted by: **Cyndi Smith**

Makes: 6 servings

Preparation: 30 minutes

Cooking: 40 minutes

Ready In: 1 hour 10 minutes

"A kind of marriage between the traditional chicken pot pie and chicken and dumplings. My family begs me to make this!"

INGREDIENTS

1/4 cup butter

2 cloves garlic, minced

1/2 cup chopped onion

1/2 cup chopped celery

1/2 cup chopped baby carrots

1/2 cup all-purpose flour

2 teaspoons white sugar

1 teaspoon salt

1 teaspoon dried basil

1/2 teaspoon ground black pepper

4 cups chicken broth

1 (10 ounce) can peas, drained

4 cups diced, cooked chicken meat

2 cups buttermilk baking mix

2 teaspoons dried basil

2/3 cup milk

DIRECTIONS

1. Preheat oven to 350°F (175°C). Lightly grease a 9x13 inch baking dish.

2. In a skillet, melt the butter over medium-high heat. Cook and stir the garlic, onion, celery, and carrots in butter until tender. Mix in the flour, sugar, salt, dried basil, and pepper. Stir in broth, and bring to a boil. Stirring constantly, boil 1 minute, reduce heat, and stir in peas. Simmer 5 minutes, then mix in chicken. Transfer mixture to the prepared baking dish.

3. In a medium bowl, combine the baking mix and 2 teaspoons dried basil. Stir in milk to form a dough. Divide the dough into 6 to 8 balls. On floured wax paper, use the palm of your hand to flatten each ball of dough into a circular shape; place on top of chicken mixture.

4. Bake in the preheated oven for 30 minutes. Cover with foil, and bake for 10 more minutes. To serve, spoon chicken mixture over biscuits.

Chicken Gruyere with Sauteed Mushrooms

Submitted by: **Rebecca**

Makes: 4 servings

Preparation: 15 minutes

Cooking: 30 minutes

Ready In: 45 minutes

"Chicken breasts are browned in butter, then baked with mushrooms, onion, and white wine. The finishing touch is an exquisite layer of melted Gruyere cheese on the top. If you enjoy rich French cooking then you will love this recipe. Serve hot over rice."

INGREDIENTS

1/4 cup all-purpose flour

1/2 teaspoon salt

1/4 teaspoon pepper

1 teaspoon chopped fresh parsley

1/2 teaspoon dried dill weed

1/4 cup butter, divided

4 boneless, skinless chicken breast halves

1 pound fresh mushrooms

1 onion, sliced into rings

1/2 cup white wine

8 ounces Gruyere cheese, shredded

DIRECTIONS

1. Preheat the oven to 350°F (175°C). In a shallow dish, stir together the flour, salt, pepper, parsley, and dill. Rinse chicken breasts, and pat dry. Dredge chicken in the flour mixture.

2. In a large skillet, heat 2 tablespoons of the butter over medium-high heat. Place chicken into the hot buttered skillet, and fry until brown on both sides. Transfer chicken breasts to a 1 quart glass baking dish. Add remaining butter to skillet, and fry the mushrooms and onion until wilted and lightly browned. Stir in the white wine, and reduce heat to medium. Simmer for 3 minutes to blend flavors. Pour the mushroom mixture over the chicken in the dish.

3. Cover dish, and bake for 20 minutes in the preheated oven. After 20 minutes, remove cover, and sprinkle with shredded cheese. Continue baking for 10 more minutes, or until cheese is lightly browned and bubbly.

Celery Wine Baked Chicken

Submitted by: **Jennifer**

Makes: 4 servings

Preparation: 20 minutes

Cooking: 1 hour 10 minutes

Ready In: 1 hour 30 minutes

"These chicken breasts are baked with a mixture of white wine, celery, sour cream, mushrooms, bell pepper, and light seasoning."

INGREDIENTS

1 tablespoon butter

¼ cup sliced fresh mushrooms

1 (10.75 ounce) can condensed cream of celery soup

¼ cup finely chopped celery

½ cup sour cream

¼ cup green bell pepper, chopped

¼ cup dry white wine

4 skinless, boneless chicken breast halves

1 pinch paprika

1 pinch garlic powder

1 pinch ground black pepper

2 teaspoons butter, divided

DIRECTIONS

1. Preheat oven to 325°F (165°C).

2. Heat 1 tablespoon butter in a small skillet over medium heat. Cook mushrooms in butter until soft.

3. In a large bowl, mix the mushrooms, soup, celery, sour cream, bell pepper, and wine. Transfer to a 9x13 inch baking dish. Top with the chicken breasts. Season with paprika, garlic powder, and pepper. Top each breast with ½ teaspoon butter.

4. Cover, and bake 1 hour in the preheated oven, or until the chicken is no longer pink and the juices run clear.

Green Bean Cheddar Chicken

Submitted by: **Marilyn G.**

Makes: 4 servings

Preparation: 15 minutes

Cooking: 40 minutes

Ready In: 55 minutes

"This is an easy to prepare, make-ahead-if-you-wish dish. All you need for accompaniment is mashed or baked potatoes, or rice. Great for company!"

INGREDIENTS

½ pound bacon

4 skinless, boneless chicken breast halves

1 tablespoon butter

20 ounces fresh green beans, washed and trimmed

1 (10.75 ounce) can condensed cream of Cheddar cheese soup

1 pinch ground cayenne pepper

½ cup seasoned dry bread crumbs

2 cups shredded Cheddar cheese

DIRECTIONS

1. Place the bacon in a skillet. Cook over medium-high heat until evenly brown. Drain, crumble, and set aside. Melt the butter in a skillet, and saute the chicken breasts 10 to 12 minutes on each side, until the exterior is golden, the meat is no longer pink, and the juices run clear.

2. Place the green beans in a saucepan with enough water to cover. Bring to a boil, and cook 5 minutes, or until tender.

3. Preheat the oven broiler. Lightly grease a 9x13 inch baking dish.

4. Arrange the beans in the bottom of the prepared baking dish. Top with the chicken, and cover evenly with the soup. Sprinkle with bread crumbs and bacon, and top with Cheddar cheese.

5. Broil 10 minutes, or until browned and bubbly.

Broccoli Chicken Divan

Submitted by: **Terry Covert**

Makes: 6 servings

Preparation: 20 minutes

Cooking: 20 minutes

Ready In: 40 minutes

"A quick and easy chicken and broccoli dish that all will love!"

INGREDIENTS

1 pound chopped fresh broccoli

1½ cups cubed, cooked chicken meat

1 (10.75 ounce) can condensed cream of broccoli soup

⅓ cup milk

½ cup shredded Cheddar cheese

1 tablespoon butter, melted

2 tablespoons dried bread crumbs

DIRECTIONS

1. Preheat oven to 450°F (230°C).

2. Place the broccoli in a saucepan with enough water to cover. Bring to a boil, and cook 5 minutes, or until tender. Drain.

3. Place the cooked broccoli in a 9 inch pie plate. Top with the chicken. In a bowl, mix the soup and milk, and pour over the chicken. Sprinkle with Cheddar cheese. Mix the melted butter with the bread crumbs, and sprinkle over the cheese.

4. Bake in the preheated oven for 15 minutes, or until bubbly and lightly brown.

Mild Cheesy Chicken Enchiladas

Submitted by: **Barbara**

Makes: 8 servings

Preparation: 30 minutes

Cooking: 30 minutes

Ready In: 1 hour

"Kids love it! Mild (not spicy) yet flavorful enchiladas featuring typical Tex-Mex flavors. Rico!"

INGREDIENTS

2 cups cubed, cooked chicken meat

1/4 cup chopped onion

4 cups shredded Cheddar cheese

1 cup sour cream

8 (8 inch) flour tortillas

1 1/2 cups chopped tomatoes

1/2 cup black olives

DIRECTIONS

1. Preheat oven to 350°F (175°C). Lightly grease a 9x13 inch baking dish.

2. In a medium bowl, mix the chicken, onion, 1 cup Cheddar cheese, and ¾ cup sour cream. Disperse the mixture evenly among the 8 tortillas. Roll into enchiladas, and arrange in single layer in the prepared baking dish.

3. In a saucepan over low heat, melt together the remaining Cheddar cheese and sour cream. Pour over the enchiladas, and top with tomatoes and olives.

4. Bake in the preheated oven for 20 to 30 minutes, or until hot and bubbly.

Layered Chicken and Black Bean Enchilada Casserole

Makes: 8 servings

Preparation: 25 minutes

Cooking: 45 minutes

Ready In: 1 hour 10 minutes

Submitted by: **Debmce4**

"Layers of sauce and tortillas mingle with a seasoned chicken and black bean mixture. This is a delicious and easy recipe best served with a side of Spanish rice. You may wish to substitute low fat sour cream."

INGREDIENTS

2 cups diced chicken breast meat

½ teaspoon ground cumin

½ teaspoon ground coriander

2 tablespoons chopped fresh cilantro

1 (15 ounce) can black beans, rinsed and drained

1 (4.5 ounce) can diced green chile peppers, drained

1 (10 ounce) can red enchilada sauce

8 (6 inch) corn tortillas

2 cups shredded Mexican blend cheese

1 (8 ounce) container sour cream

DIRECTIONS

1. Preheat the oven to 375°F (190°C).

2. Heat a large skillet over medium heat, and spray with vegetable cooking spray. Saute chicken with cumin and coriander until chicken is cooked through. Transfer to a medium bowl. Stir in the cilantro, black beans, and green chile peppers.

3. Spread half of the enchilada sauce over the bottom of an 11x7 inch baking dish. Place 4 tortillas over the sauce, overlapping if necessary. Spoon half of the chicken mixture over the tortillas, and sprinkle with half of the cheese and half of the sour cream. Spoon the remaining enchilada sauce over the cheese, and make another layer of tortillas. Layer the remaining chicken mixture over the tortillas. Cover dish with a lid or aluminum foil.

4. Bake for 30 minutes in the preheated oven. Remove the cover, and sprinkle the remaining cheese over the top and dot with sour cream. Continue cooking, uncovered, for an additional 5 to 10 minutes, or until cheese melts. Let stand 10 minutes before serving.

main dish - seafood

Cheesy Baked Seafood Au Gratin, Mexican Baked Fish, or Fisherman's Catch Chowder are perfect any night of the week – especially if you have a fisherman at home filling the freezer with fresh fillets. Or, you may want to enjoy the warm southern flavors of crawfish and jambalaya on a cold winter's eve. You can even try a new recipe for the classic tuna casserole — a standby seafood supper that couldn't be easier.

Fisherman's Catch Chowder

Submitted by: **Corwynn Darkholme**

Makes: 4 servings

Preparation: 15 minutes

Cooking: 8 hours

Ready In: 8 hours 15 minutes

"This is a very savory fish chowder, and anyone who is a seafood lover will love this recipe! Use any combinations of the following fish: halibut, flounder, ocean perch, pike, rainbow trout, or haddock. (Double recipe for 5-quart slow cooker.)"

INGREDIENTS

1½ pounds cod fillets, cubed

1 (16 ounce) can whole peeled tomatoes, mashed

1 (8 ounce) jar clam juice

½ cup chopped onion

½ cup chopped celery

½ cup chopped carrots

½ cup dry white wine

¼ cup chopped fresh parsley

¼ teaspoon dried rosemary

1 teaspoon salt

3 tablespoons all-purpose flour

3 tablespoons butter, melted

⅓ cup light cream

DIRECTIONS

1. In a slow cooker, stir together the cod, tomatoes, clam juice, onion, celery, carrots, wine, parsley, rosemary, and salt. Cover, and cook on Low 7 to 8 hours or on High 3 to 4 hours.

2. One hour prior to serving, mix flour, butter, and light cream in a small bowl. Stir into the slow cooker until the fish mixture is thickened.

Quick and Easy Clam Chowder

Submitted by: **Deena**

Makes: 8 to 10 servi

Preparation: 10 minute

Cooking: 8 hours

Ready In: 8 hours 10 minutes

"The best ever clam chowder you have ever tasted, and it is easy and fast. You will pass this recipe along to your family and friends. If you like more clams you can always add more. Sometimes I will also cube potatoes and throw them in."

INGREDIENTS

1 (10.75 ounce) can condensed cream of celery soup

1 (10.75 ounce) can condensed cream of potato soup

1 (10.75 ounce) can New England clam chowder

2 (6.5 ounce) cans minced clams

1 quart half-and-half cream

1 pint heavy whipping cream

DIRECTIONS

1. Mix cream of celery soup, cream of potato soup, clam chowder, 1 can undrained clams, 1 can drained clams, half-and-half cream, and whipping cream into a slow cooker.

2. Cover, and cook on low for 6 to 8 hours.

mbalaya

ela Quinn

Something for that day you just don't really want to cook but want to use a slow cooker."

INGREDIENTS

1 pound boneless, skinless chicken thighs, cut into 2-inch pieces

2 stalks celery, thinly sliced

1 medium green bell pepper, cut into 1 inch pieces

1 medium onion, chopped

2 cloves garlic, minced

1 (28 ounce) can crushed tomatoes, with liquid

1 tablespoon white sugar

1/2 teaspoon salt

1/2 teaspoon dried Italian seasoning

1/4 teaspoon cayenne pepper

1 bay leaf

1 cup uncooked orzo pasta

1 pound cooked shrimp, peeled and deveined

DIRECTIONS

1. In a slow cooker, mix chicken, celery, green bell pepper, onion, garlic, tomatoes with liquid, sugar, salt, Italian seasoning, cayenne pepper, and bay leaf. Cover, and cook on Low 7 to 9 hours.

2. Remove bay leaf from the chicken mixture, and stir in orzo. Increase heat to High. Cook 15 minutes, until orzo is tender.

3. Stir in shrimp, and cook 2 minutes, until shrimp are heated through.

Mexican Baked Fish

Submitted by: **Christine Johnson**

Makes: 6 servings

Preparation: 15 minutes

Cooking: 15 minutes

Ready In: 30 minutes

"A baked fish dish. You get to choose the heat. Use mild salsa for a little heat and extra hot salsa for lots of heat! Serve with rice, black beans, warm tortillas and lime Margaritas for a festive meal!"

INGREDIENTS

1½ pounds cod

1 cup salsa

1 cup shredded sharp Cheddar cheese

½ cup coarsely crushed corn chips

1 avocado - peeled, pitted and sliced

¼ cup sour cream

DIRECTIONS

1. Preheat oven to 400°F (200°C). Lightly grease one 8x12 inch baking dish.

2. Rinse fish fillets under cold water, and pat dry with paper towels. Lay fillets side by side in the prepared baking dish. Pour the salsa over the top, and sprinkle evenly with the shredded cheese. Top with the crushed corn chips.

3. Bake, uncovered, in the preheated oven for 15 minutes, or until fish is opaque and flakes with a fork. Serve topped with sliced avocado and sour cream.

Haddock Bubbly Bake

Submitted by: **Susan**

Makes: 6 servings

Preparation: 10 minutes

Cooking: 40 minutes

Ready In: 50 minutes

"This is really great served with mashed potatoes and peas or veggie of your choice. This dish is a favorite of Nova Scotia, Canada."

INGREDIENTS

2 pounds haddock fillets

salt and pepper to taste

1 (10.75 ounce) can condensed cream of mushroom soup

1 onion, thinly sliced

1 cup shredded mild Cheddar cheese

DIRECTIONS

1. Preheat oven to 350°F (175°C). Lightly butter a 2 quart casserole dish.

2. Arrange fish fillets in the bottom of the prepared casserole dish, and sprinkle with salt and pepper to taste. Layer onion slices over fish. Spread cream of mushroom soup over all, and top with shredded cheese.

3. Bake in preheated oven for about 40 minutes, or until bubbly and fish flakes easily with a fork.

Cod au Gratin

Submitted by: **Rose Small**

Makes: 6 servings

Preparation: 20 minutes

Cooking: 25 minutes

Ready In: 45 minutes

"If you want to impress a Newfoundlander, do it with simple goodness. This recipe is straight from Newfoundland!"

INGREDIENTS

2 pounds cod fillets

3 tablespoons margarine

6 tablespoons all-purpose flour

2 cups milk

salt and ground black pepper to taste

1½ cups shredded Cheddar cheese

DIRECTIONS

1. Preheat oven to 350°F (175°C). Grease an 8x12 inch baking dish. Bring a large pot of lightly salted water to a boil. Add cod fillets and cook for 4 to 6 minutes; drain.

2. Melt margarine in a medium saucepan. Remove from heat and mix in the flour and milk. Return to stove over medium heat, and stir until thickened. Season with salt and pepper.

3. Flake fish into baking dish, alternating layers with sauce. Sprinkle top with shredded cheese.

4. Bake in preheated oven for 20 to 25 minutes, or until cheese is browned.

Baked Seafood Au Gratin

Submitted by: **Katy B. Minchew**

Makes: 8 servings

Preparation: 20 minutes

Cooking: 1 hour

Ready In: 1 hour 20 minutes

"This was my Mom's favorite seafood recipe, she is now 88, I am 60 and this is my all time favorite seafood recipe also. I have had guests, who, when invited to dinner, specifically request this to be served."

INGREDIENTS

1 onion, chopped

1 green bell pepper, chopped

1 cup butter, divided

1 cup all-purpose flour, divided

1 pound fresh crabmeat

4 cups water

1 pound fresh shrimp, peeled and deveined

½ pound small scallops

½ pound flounder fillets

3 cups milk

1 cup shredded sharp Cheddar cheese

1 tablespoon distilled white vinegar

1 teaspoon Worcestershire sauce

½ teaspoon salt

1 pinch ground black pepper

1 dash hot pepper sauce

½ cup grated Parmesan cheese

DIRECTIONS

1. In a heavy skillet, saute the onion and the pepper in ½ cup of butter. Cook until tender. Mix in ½ cup of the flour, and cook over medium heat for 10 minutes, stirring frequently. Stir in crabmeat, remove from heat, and set aside.

2. In a large Dutch oven, bring the water to a boil. Add the shrimp, scallops, and flounder, and simmer for 3 minutes. Drain, reserving 1 cup of the cooking liquid, and set the seafood aside.

3. In a heavy saucepan, melt the remaining ½ cup butter over low heat. Stir in remaining ½ cup flour. Cook and stir constantly for 1 minute. Gradually add the milk plus the 1 cup reserved cooking liquid. Raise heat to medium; cook, stirring constantly, until the mixture is thickened and bubbly. Mix in the shredded Cheddar cheese, vinegar, Worcestershire sauce, salt, pepper, and hot sauce. Stir in cooked seafood.

4. Preheat oven to 350°F (175°C). Lightly grease one 9x13 inch baking dish. Press crabmeat mixture into the bottom of the prepared pan. Spoon the seafood mixture over the crabmeat crust, and sprinkle with the Parmesan cheese.

5. Bake in the preheated oven for 30 minutes, or until lightly browned. Serve immediately.

Deb's Scallops Florentine

Submitted by: **Debra Connors**

Makes: 6 servings

Preparation: 30 minutes

Cooking: 25 minutes

Ready In: 55 minutes

"Mouthwatering scallops and spinach, topped off with a rich Parmesan cheese sauce, baked until bubbly and delicious!"

INGREDIENTS

1 pound sea scallops

3 tablespoons butter

2 tablespoons all-purpose flour

1 cup heavy cream

¼ cup grated Parmesan cheese

salt to taste

ground black pepper to taste

1 (10 ounce) package frozen chopped spinach, thawed

1 cup shredded mozzarella cheese

¼ cup grated Parmesan cheese

¼ cup plain bread crumbs

1 tablespoon OLD BAY® Seasoning

DIRECTIONS

1. Preheat oven to 350°F (175°C). Lightly grease a 9 inch pie plate.

2. Bring a pot of water to a rolling boil. Rinse the scallops, and drop them into the boiling water; cook for 2 minutes. Remove the scallops with a slotted spoon, and pat dry. Place on the bottom of the prepared pie plate.

3. In a small saucepan, melt the butter, and stir in the flour. Cook over low heat for 3 minutes. Whisk in heavy cream and ¼ cup Parmesan cheese. Season with salt and pepper to taste. Cook for another 2 to 3 minutes, stirring constantly, or until thick.

4. Squeeze the spinach dry, and spread over the scallops. Pour the cream sauce over the spinach, and top with mozzarella cheese, ¼ cup Parmesan cheese, and bread crumbs. Sprinkle Old Bay Seasoning over the bread crumbs.

5. Bake in preheated oven for 15 minutes, or until browned and bubbly.

Crawfish Fettuccine

Submitted by: **Cynthia**

Makes: 8 servings

Preparation: 15 minutes

Cooking: 1 hour 15 minutes

Ready In: 1 hour 30 minutes

"One word — delicious! This creamy dish will leave them begging for more. The crawfish and Cajun seasonings give a new twist to fettuccine."

INGREDIENTS

6 tablespoons butter

1 large onion, chopped

1 green bell pepper, chopped

3 stalks celery, chopped

1 clove garlic, minced

1 tablespoon all-purpose flour

1 pound peeled crawfish tails

1 (8 ounce) package processed cheese food

1 cup half-and-half cream

2 teaspoons Cajun seasoning

2 teaspoons cayenne pepper

1 pound dry fettuccine pasta

1/2 cup grated Parmesan cheese

DIRECTIONS

1. Melt the butter in a large skillet over medium heat. Cook onion, bell pepper, celery, and garlic in butter until onions are tender. Stir in flour, and cook for 5 to 10 minutes, stirring frequently. Stir in crawfish. Cover, and simmer for 15 to 20 minutes, stirring often.

2. Stir in the processed cheese, half-and-half, Cajun seasonings, and cayenne pepper. Cover, and simmer for about 20 minutes, stirring occasionally.

3. Meanwhile, bring a large pot of lightly salted water to a boil. Cook pasta in boiling water for 8 to 10 minutes, or until al dente; drain.

4. Preheat oven to 350°F (175°C). Butter a 9x13 inch baking dish. Stir noodles into crawfish mixture; pour into prepared dish, and sprinkle with Parmesan cheese.

5. Bake in a preheated oven for 20 minutes, or until hot and bubbly.

Seafood Lasagna II

Submitted by: **Rayna Jordan**

Makes: 8 servings

Preparation: 30 minutes

Cooking: 1 hour

Ready In: 1 hour 30 minutes

"I improved on a friends recipe...now it is the best I ever cooked or tasted!"

INGREDIENTS

9 lasagna noodles

1 tablespoon butter

1 cup minced onion

1 (8 ounce) package cream cheese, softened

1½ cups cottage cheese

1 egg, beaten

2 teaspoons dried basil leaves

½ teaspoon salt

⅛ teaspoon freshly ground black pepper

2 (10.75 ounce) cans condensed cream of mushroom soup

⅓ cup milk

⅓ cup dry white wine

1 (6 ounce) can crabmeat, drained and flaked

1 pound cooked small shrimp

¼ cup grated Parmesan cheese

½ cup shredded sharp Cheddar cheese

DIRECTIONS

1. Bring a pot of lightly salted water to a boil. Cook pasta for 8 to 10 minutes, or until al dente; drain, and rinse in cold water. Preheat oven to 350°F (175°C).

2. In a skillet, cook onion in butter over medium heat until tender. Remove from heat, and stir in cream cheese, cottage cheese, egg, basil, and salt and pepper.

3. In a medium bowl, mix together the soup, milk, wine, crabmeat, and shrimp.

4. Lay 3 cooked lasagna noodles on the bottom of a 9x13 inch baking dish. Spread ⅓ of the onion mixture over the noodles. Then spread ⅓ of the soup mixture over the onion layer. Repeat the noodle, onion, soup layers twice more. Top with Cheddar cheese and Parmesan cheese.

5. Bake in preheated oven for 45 minutes, or until heated through and bubbly.

Hearty Tuna Casserole

Submitted by: **Ann L.**

Makes: 6 servings

Preparation: 15 minutes

Cooking: 45 minutes

Ready In: 1 hour

"This isn't your Grandma's tuna casserole, but it is sure to please everybody in the family."

INGREDIENTS

3 cups uncooked egg noodles

2 (6 ounce) cans tuna, drained

1/2 cup chopped celery

1/3 cup chopped green onions

1/3 cup sour cream

2 teaspoons prepared mustard

1/2 cup mayonnaise

1/2 teaspoon dried thyme

1/4 teaspoon salt

1 small zucchini, sliced

1 cup shredded Monterey Jack cheese

1 tomato, chopped

DIRECTIONS

1. Preheat oven to 350°F (175°C). Grease a 2 quart casserole dish.

2. Bring a large pot of salted water to a boil, add noodles, and cook until al dente; drain.

3. In a large mixing bowl, combine noodles, tuna, celery, and green onion. Stir in sour cream, mustard, and mayonnaise. Season with salt and thyme. Spoon ½ of the noodle mixture into the prepared casserole dish. Arrange a layer of zucchini over the mixture. Top with the remaining noodles, followed by a layer of zucchini. Top the entire casserole with cheese.

4. Bake in preheated oven for 30 minutes, or until hot and bubbly. Sprinkle the casserole with tomatoes before serving.

Tuna Noodle Casserole

Submitted by: **Cat**

Makes: 6 servings

Preparation: 10 minutes

Cooking: 50 minutes

Ready In: 1 hour

"This is easy, filling, and can be quick if you omit the baking step, which I often do."

INGREDIENTS

1 (8 ounce) package wide egg noodles

2 tablespoons butter

2 tablespoons all-purpose flour

1 teaspoon salt (optional)

1 cup milk

1 cup shredded sharp Cheddar cheese

1 (6 ounce) can tuna, drained

1 (15 ounce) can peas, drained

DIRECTIONS

1. Preheat oven to 350°F (175°C). Coat a 2 quart casserole dish with cooking spray.

2. In a large pot of salted water, boil noodles until al dente. Drain well.

3. In a medium saucepan, combine flour, butter, and salt. Stir until butter is melted and ingredients are combined evenly. Add milk, and whisk until the sauce thickens (usually it is at the proper consistency by the time it begins to boil). Add cheese to mixture, and whisk until cheese is melted and mixture is well blended. Stir in tuna, peas, and noodles. Spread evenly in prepared dish.

4. Bake in preheated oven for 30 minutes.

Tuna Noodle Casserole II

Submitted by: **Chris Smith**

Makes: 8 servings

Preparation: 10 minutes

Cooking: 50 minutes

Ready In: 1 hour

"This is the old tried and true, 1950's style tuna noodle casserole we remember as kids. Uses ingredients most people have on hand, especially those broken chips at the bottom of the bag that nobody wants to eat. Got to have those chips on top to be real."

INGREDIENTS

1 (16 ounce) package uncooked pasta shells

2 (6 ounce) cans tuna, drained

1 (10.75 ounce) can condensed cream of mushroom soup

1 (10.75 ounce) can condensed cream of celery soup

1¼ cups milk

1 teaspoon salt

¼ teaspoon ground black pepper

1 teaspoon crushed garlic

4 slices processed American cheese

1½ cups crushed potato chips

DIRECTIONS

1. Boil pasta in lightly salted water for 10 minutes, or until al dente; drain well. Return the pasta to the pot it was cooked in.

2. Preheat oven to 350°F (175°C). Spray a 2½ quart casserole dish with cooking spray.

3. Mix tuna with cream of mushroom soup, cream of celery soup, milk, salt, black pepper, and garlic in a medium saucepan. Place pan over medium low heat, and heat through. Alternatively, place these ingredients in a microwave safe dish, and warm in the microwave.

4. Mix tuna mixture with pasta. Spread ½ of the noodles into the prepared dish. Arrange the cheese slices over the noodles, then spread the remaining noodle mixture over the cheese. Top with crushed potato chips.

5. Bake, uncovered, for 20 to 30 minutes; cook until the casserole is hot, and the chips begin to brown. Let cool for 10 minutes before serving.

Easy Tuna Casserole

Submitted by: **Lindsay**

Makes: 8 servings

Preparation: 15 minutes

Cooking: 30 minutes

Ready In: 45 minutes

"Tuna, macaroni, creamy soup, cheese and fried onions are all you need to make this super easy tuna casserole that I learned from my roommate. It's great as leftovers, too."

INGREDIENTS

3 cups cooked macaroni

1 (6 ounce) can tuna, drained

1 (10.75 ounce) can condensed cream of chicken soup

1 cup shredded Cheddar cheese

1½ cups French fried onions

DIRECTIONS

1. Preheat oven to 350°F (175°C).

2. In a 9x13-inch baking dish, combine the macaroni, tuna, and soup. Mix well, and then top with cheese.

3. Bake at 350°F (175°C) for about 25 minutes, or until bubbly. Sprinkle with fried onions, and bake for another 5 minutes. Serve hot.

meatless mains

Flavor is the main ingredient in these spicy, sassy dishes featuring an array of vegetables, as well as beans, cheese, and pasta. Try making zesty lasagna, a robust black bean chili, or a delicious veggie enchilada casserole at your next get-together. These fabulously filling main dishes are a great way to take a break from the standard meat-based meal.

Beezie's Black Bean Soup

Submitted by: **Beezie**

Makes: 10 servings

Preparation: 1 hour

Cooking: 5 hours

Ready In: 6 hours

*"This soup has gained rave reviews from my non-veggie friends and family! It's
bursting with healthy goodness, never mind that it tastes so wonderfully yummy!
The soup loves to change, if you're cleaning out your refrigerator, be creative..."*

INGREDIENTS

1 pound dry black beans

1½ quarts water

1 carrot, chopped

1 stalk celery, chopped

1 large red onion, chopped

6 cloves garlic, crushed

2 green bell peppers, chopped

2 jalapeno pepper, seeded and minced

¼ cup dry lentils

1 (28 ounce) can peeled and diced tomatoes

2 tablespoons chili powder

2 teaspoons ground cumin

½ teaspoon dried oregano

½ teaspoon ground black pepper

3 tablespoons red wine vinegar

1 tablespoon salt

½ cup uncooked white rice

DIRECTIONS

1. In a large pot over medium-high heat, place the beans in three times their volume of water. Bring to a boil, and let boil 10 minutes. Cover, remove from heat and let stand 1 hour. Drain, and rinse.

2. In a slow cooker, combine soaked beans and 1½ quarts fresh water. Cover, and cook for 3 hours on High.

3. Stir in carrot, celery, onion, garlic, bell peppers, jalapeno pepper, lentils, and tomatoes. Season with chili powder, cumin, oregano, black pepper, red wine vinegar, and salt. Cook on Low for 2 to 3 hours. Stir the rice into the slow cooker in the last 20 minutes of cooking.

4. Puree about half of the soup with a blender or food processor, then pour back into the pot before serving.

Spicy Slow Cooker Black Bean Soup

Submitted by: **Lynn Eberle**

Makes: 6 servings

Preparation: 5 minutes

Ready In: 6 hours 5 minutes

"This soup can be served as is or run through the blender for a creamy version. You can adjust the spice to cool it down."

INGREDIENTS

1 pound dry black beans, soaked overnight

4 teaspoons diced jalapeno peppers

6 cups chicken broth

1/2 teaspoon garlic powder

1 tablespoon chili powder

1 teaspoon ground cumin

1 teaspoon cayenne pepper

3/4 teaspoon ground black pepper

1/2 teaspoon hot pepper sauce

DIRECTIONS

1. Drain black beans, and rinse.

2. Combine beans, jalapenos, and chicken broth in a slow cooker. Season with garlic powder, chili powder, cumin, cayenne, pepper, and hot pepper sauce.

3. Cook on High for 4 hours. Reduce heat to Low, and continue cooking for 2 hours, or until you are ready to eat.

Grandma's Slow Cooker Vegetarian Chili

Submitted by: **Kevin S. Weiss**

Makes: 8 servings

Preparation: 10 minutes

Cooking: 2 hours

Ready In: 2 hours 10 minutes

"This is a simple crowd pleasing recipe that can sit in a slow cooker until it is time to serve."

INGREDIENTS

1 (19 ounce) can black bean soup

1 (15 ounce) can kidney beans, rinsed and drained

1 (15 ounce) can garbanzo beans, rinsed and drained

1 (16 ounce) can vegetarian baked beans

1 (14.5 ounce) can chopped tomatoes in puree

1 (15 ounce) can whole kernel corn, drained

1 onion, chopped

1 green bell pepper, chopped

2 stalks celery, chopped

2 cloves garlic, chopped

1 tablespoon chili powder, or to taste

1 tablespoon dried parsley

1 tablespoon dried oregano

1 tablespoon dried basil

DIRECTIONS

1. In a slow cooker, combine black bean soup, kidney beans, garbanzo beans, baked beans, tomatoes, corn, onion, bell pepper and celery. Season with garlic, chili powder, parsley, oregano and basil. Cook for at least two hours on High.

Creamy Slow Cooker Potato Cheese Soup

Submitted by: **Kathy Byers**

Makes: 18 servings

Preparation: 30 minutes

Cooking: 5 hours

Ready In: 5 hours 30 minutes

"Soup for a crowd made in my 6 ½ quart slow cooker. Hearty and flavorful. Serve with corn bread or your favorite crusty bread and a salad or other vegetable. For a 3 quart slow cooker, halve all ingredient amounts."

INGREDIENTS

¼ cup butter

½ white onion, chopped

¼ cup all-purpose flour

2 cups water

2 large carrots, diced

4 stalks celery, diced

1 tablespoon dried, minced garlic

salt and pepper to taste

1 cup milk

2 tablespoons chicken soup base

1 cup warm water

5 pounds russet potatoes, peeled and cubed

1 bay leaf

1 cup shredded Cheddar cheese

6 slices crisp cooked bacon, crumbled

DIRECTIONS

1. Melt butter in a large saucepan over medium heat. Cook onion in butter until translucent. Stir in flour until smooth, then gradually stir in 2 cups water, carrots, celery, garlic, salt, and pepper. Heat through, then stir in milk. Dissolve chicken base in 1 cup warm water, and pour into vegetable mixture.

2. Place potatoes in slow cooker, and pour heated vegetable mixture into potatoes. Place bay leaf in pot.

3. Cover, and cook 5 hours on High, or 8 hours on Low.

4. Remove bay leaf. Puree about 4 cups of the soup in a blender or food processor, and then stir pureed soup into contents of slow cooker. Stir in cheese and bacon until cheese is melted.

Slow Cooker Mediterranean Stew

Submitted by: **Lisa Bromfield**

Makes: 10 servings

Preparation: 30 minutes

Cooking: 10 hours

Ready In: 10 hours 30 minutes

"A nice hearty stew that is wicked easy."

INGREDIENTS

1 butternut squash - peeled, seeded, and cubed

2 cups cubed eggplant, with peel

2 cups cubed zucchini

1 (10 ounce) package frozen okra, thawed

1 (8 ounce) can tomato sauce

1 cup chopped onion

1 ripe tomato, chopped

1 carrot, sliced thin

1/2 cup vegetable broth

1/3 cup raisins

1 clove garlic, chopped

1/2 teaspoon ground cumin

1/2 teaspoon ground turmeric

1/4 teaspoon crushed red pepper

1/4 teaspoon ground cinnamon

1/4 teaspoon paprika

DIRECTIONS

1. In a slow cooker, combine butternut squash, eggplant, zucchini, okra, tomato sauce, onion, tomato, carrot, broth, raisins, and garlic. Season with cumin, turmeric, red pepper, cinnamon, and paprika.

2. Cover, and cook on Low for 8 to 10 hours, or until vegetables are tender.

Hearty Vegetable Lasagna

Submitted by: **Sue**

Makes: 12 servings

Preparation: 25 minutes

Cooking: 1 hour

Ready In: 1 hour 40 minutes

"This hearty, vegetable lasagna is the only lasagna my husband will eat. We love it!!! Hope you all enjoy as much as we do."

INGREDIENTS

1 (16 ounce) package lasagna noodles

1 pound fresh mushrooms, sliced

3/4 cup chopped green bell pepper

3/4 cup chopped onion

3 cloves garlic, minced

2 tablespoons vegetable oil

2 (26 ounce) jars pasta sauce

1 teaspoon dried basil

1 (15 ounce) container part-skim ricotta cheese

4 cups shredded mozzarella cheese

2 eggs

1/2 cup grated Parmesan cheese

DIRECTIONS

1. Cook the lasagna noodles in a large pot of boiling water for 10 minutes, or until al dente. Rinse with cold water, and drain.

2. In a large saucepan, cook and stir mushrooms, green peppers, onion, and garlic in oil. Stir in pasta sauce and basil; bring to a boil. Reduce heat, and simmer 15 minutes.

3. Mix together ricotta, 2 cups mozzarella cheese, and eggs.

4. Preheat oven to 350°F (175°C). Spread 1 cup tomato sauce into the bottom of a greased 9x13 inch baking dish. Layer 1/2 each, lasagna noodles, ricotta mix, sauce, and Parmesan cheese. Repeat layering, and top with remaining 2 cups mozzarella cheese.

5. Bake, uncovered, for 40 minutes. Let stand 15 minutes before serving.

Spicy Vegetarian Lasagna

Submitted by: **Randi DeWeese**

Makes: 12 servings

Preparation: 30 minutes

Cooking: 1 hour 10 minutes

Ready In: 1 hour 40 minutes

"A colorful and tasty veggie lasagna with plenty of peppers and cheese, with red pepper flakes for zip."

INGREDIENTS

1 (16 ounce) package lasagna noodles

2 teaspoons olive oil

2/3 cup diced red bell pepper

2/3 cup diced orange bell pepper

2/3 cup diced yellow bell pepper

2/3 cup diced green bell pepper

1 small yellow onion, diced

2 (14.5 ounce) cans diced tomatoes

1 (6 ounce) can tomato paste

1½ cups water

1 dash crushed red pepper flakes

¼ cup grated Parmesan cheese

1 (15 ounce) container ricotta cheese

1 (8 ounce) package shredded mozzarella cheese

4 eggs

¼ teaspoon black pepper

¼ teaspoon dried oregano, crushed

¼ cup grated Parmesan cheese (optional)

DIRECTIONS

1. Bring a large pot of lightly salted water to a boil. Cook lasagna pasta in boiling water for 8 to 10 minutes, or until al dente. Drain, rinse with cold water, and place on wax paper to cool.

2. Cook bell peppers and onion in olive oil in a large sauce pan until onions are translucent. Stir in diced tomatoes, tomato paste, water, and red pepper flakes. More red pepper flakes can be added if spicier sauce is preferred. Simmer for 30 minutes.

3. Preheat oven to 375 °F (190°C). In a medium bowl, combine Parmesan cheese, ricotta cheese, mozzarella cheese, eggs, black pepper, and oregano.

4. Place a small amount of sauce in the bottom of a 9x13 inch baking dish. Reserve ½ cup of the sauce. Place three lasagna noodles lengthwise in pan. Layer some of the cheese mixture and the vegetable sauce on top of noodles. Repeat layering with remaining ingredients, ending with noodles. Spread reserved sauce over top of noodles. Sprinkle with grated Parmesan cheese, if desired.

5. Cover dish with foil, and bake for 40 minutes or until bubbly. Remove foil during last 10 minutes of baking.

Veggie Lasagna Florentine

Submitted by: **Denise Smith**

Makes: 12 servings

Preparation: 20 minutes

Cooking: 1 hour 25 minutes

Ready In: 1 hour 45 minutes

"This is a recipe I created for my vegetarian sister-in-law after she ran the Marine Corp Marathon in Washington, DC. I was not able to be there to cheer her on so I sent this dish. It is actually better the next day but I have never been able to keep my family out of it once they smell the aroma!"

INGREDIENTS

1 (16 ounce) package lasagna noodles

2 tablespoons olive oil

1 onion, chopped

1 (8 ounce) can sliced mushrooms

2 tablespoons minced garlic

1 zucchini, finely chopped

2 (28 ounce) cans crushed tomatoes

1 (6 ounce) can tomato paste

1 tablespoon dried oregano

1 pinch brown sugar

salt to taste

1 (10 ounce) package frozen chopped spinach, thawed

1 (16 ounce) container nonfat cottage cheese

2 eggs

3 tablespoons dried basil, divided

¼ cup grated Parmesan cheese

1 pound shredded mozzarella cheese

DIRECTIONS

1. Cook lasagna noodles in a large pot of lightly salted, boiling water for 10 minutes, or until al dente. Rinse with cool water, drain, and set aside.

2. Heat oil in a large skillet over medium heat. Cook the chopped onions, mushrooms, garlic, and zucchini in the oil until soft. Stir in both cans of crushed tomatoes, tomato paste, oregano, brown sugar, and salt to taste. Reduce heat to low, and simmer for 15 minutes.

3. Meanwhile, microwave frozen spinach until cooked. Cool, and then squeeze out excess water. Drain cottage cheese. Using a mixer, blend spinach, cottage cheese, eggs, and 2 tablespoons basil until smooth. In a separate bowl, combine shredded mozzarella cheese and grated Parmesan cheese.

4. Preheat oven to 350°F (175°C). Spread 1 cup sauce in the bottom of a 9x13 inch baking dish. Layer ⅓ of the noodles, ⅓ cottage cheese/spinach mixture, ⅓ of remaining sauce, and ⅓ cheese mixture. Repeat layers with remaining ingredients. Sprinkle top with remaining 1 tablespoon of dried basil.

5. Bake in preheated oven for 60 minutes. Let stand for 10 minutes before serving.

Kalamata Olive, Tomato, and Cheese Melt

Submitted by: **Cindy Doerksen**

Makes: 6 servings

Preparation: 15 minutes

Cooking: 40 minutes

Ready In: 55 minutes

"Rotini pasta is tossed with tomatoes, kalamata olives, and peppers, topped with feta and Cheddar cheeses, and baked until golden brown and bubbly. Delicious."

INGREDIENTS

1 (16 ounce) package rotini pasta

2 tablespoons olive oil

1 small onion, chopped

1 jalapeno pepper, chopped

1/2 medium green bell pepper, chopped

1 (28 ounce) can diced tomatoes

1/2 cup red wine

20 kalamata olives, pitted and chopped

2/3 cup crumbled feta cheese

2/3 cup shredded reduced-fat Cheddar cheese

DIRECTIONS

1. Preheat oven to 350°F (175°C). Bring a large pot of lightly salted water to a boil. Add pasta, cook for 8 to 10 minutes, until al dente, and drain.

2. Heat oil in a large heavy skillet over medium heat. Saute onion, jalapeno, and green bell pepper until onions are soft and translucent. Stir in tomatoes, wine, and kalamata olives. Simmer 15 minutes. Toss pasta with sauce until evenly coated. Pour into a 9x13 inch baking dish. Sprinkle with feta cheese and Cheddar cheese.

3. Bake 5 minutes in the preheated oven. Set oven to broiler setting. Broil for 5 minutes, or until topping is golden brown and bubbly.

Cheryl's Spinach Cheesy Pasta Casserole

Submitted by: **Faye Berlage**

Makes: 12 servings
Preparation: 15 minutes
Cooking: 1 hour
Ready In: 1 hour 15 minutes

"This recipe was given by a friend and it instantly became a favorite! It tastes great as leftovers as well! Enjoy!"

INGREDIENTS

1 (12 ounce) package medium seashell pasta

1 (10 ounce) package frozen chopped spinach, thawed

2 eggs

¼ cup olive oil

½ cup bread crumbs

1½ (26 ounce) jars tomato basil pasta sauce

1 (8 ounce) package shredded Cheddar cheese

1 (8 ounce) package shredded mozzarella cheese

DIRECTIONS

1. Preheat oven to 350°F (175°C).

2. Bring a large pot of lightly salted water to a boil. Cook pasta in boiling water for 8 to 10 minutes, or until al dente; drain. Bring ½ cup water to a boil in a saucepan, and cook the spinach 4 to 6 minutes, until tender.

3. Place the cooked pasta in a medium bowl. In a small bowl, whisk together the eggs and oil. Toss the pasta with the cooked spinach, egg mixture, and bread crumbs.

4. Cover the bottom of a 9x13 inch baking dish with ⅓ of the pasta sauce. Pour half of the pasta mixture into the baking dish, and cover with another ⅓ of the pasta sauce. Sprinkle with half of the Cheddar cheese and half of the mozzarella. Layer with remaining pasta mixture, and top with remaining sauce. Sprinkle with the rest of the Cheddar and mozzarella cheeses.

5. Bake 45 minutes in the preheated oven, or until bubbly and lightly browned.

Cheesy Spinach Casserole

Submitted by: **Becki Dakan**

Makes: 4 servings

Preparation: 10 minutes

Cooking: 40 minutes

Ready In: 50 minutes

"A wonderful dish for parties or for home. This dish has a strong spinach and Monterey Jack cheese flavor, with a hint of artichoke and onion."

INGREDIENTS

6 ounces uncooked spaghetti

1 egg

¼ cup milk

½ cup sour cream

1 (10 ounce) package frozen chopped spinach, thawed

½ (14 ounce) can artichoke hearts, drained and chopped

1 (8 ounce) package shredded Monterey Jack cheese

4 tablespoons grated Parmesan cheese, divided

1 teaspoon dried minced onion

salt and pepper to taste

paprika to taste

DIRECTIONS

1. Bring a large pot of lightly salted water to a boil. Cook spaghetti in boiling water for 8 to 10 minutes, or until al dente; drain. Preheat oven to 350°F (175°C).

2. In a 2 quart casserole dish, whisk together egg, milk, and sour cream. Using a wooden spoon, stir in spinach, artichoke hearts, Monterey Jack cheese, 2 tablespoons Parmesan cheese, and cooked spaghetti. Season with minced onion, salt, and pepper. Top with a sprinkling of paprika and remaining Parmesan cheese.

3. Cover, and bake in preheated oven for 15 minutes. Remove cover, and bake for another 15 minutes. Let stand 2 minutes before serving.

Spinach Veggie Casserole

Submitted by: Leslie Gurowitz

Makes: 8 servings

Preparation: 25 minutes

Cooking: 50 minutes

Ready In: 1 hour 15 minutes

"Lots of spinach, lots of rice and lots of cheese in this hearty casserole. Very tasty and hearty main course."

INGREDIENTS

1¾ cups water

¾ cup white rice

3 tablespoons butter

3 tablespoons all-purpose flour

2 cups milk

2 cups shredded Swiss cheese

salt and pepper to taste

1 teaspoon hot pepper sauce

2 (10 ounce) packages frozen chopped spinach, thawed and drained

2 tablespoons vegetable oil

1 onion, chopped

2 cloves garlic

1 red bell pepper, chopped

1 (15 ounce) can white corn, drained

½ cup dried bread crumbs, seasoned

2 tablespoons butter, diced

DIRECTIONS

1. Combine water and rice in a small saucepan, and bring to a boil. Cover, reduce heat, and simmer for 20 minutes.

2. Melt 3 tablespoons butter in a large saucepan over medium heat. Mix flour into the butter slowly, stirring constantly. Whisk in milk a small amount at time until smooth. Cook over a medium heat until thickened, stirring constantly. Stir in 1½ cups shredded Swiss cheese, salt, pepper, and hot sauce; stir until the cheese melts. Stir in spinach.

3. Meanwhile, heat oil in a skillet over medium heat. Cook onion, garlic, bell pepper, and corn in oil until tender, stirring frequently.

4. Preheat oven to 350°F (175°C). In a large casserole dish, combine rice, spinach-cheese mixture, and onion mixture. Sprinkle breadcrumbs over the top of the casserole, dot with 2 tablespoons butter, and top with remaining ½ cup of cheese.

5. Bake, uncovered, in the preheated oven for approximately 20 minutes, or until cheese topping melts.

Easy Mashed Potato and Roasted Vegetable Enchiladas

Submitted by: **Letty**

Makes: 12 servings

Preparation: 40 minutes

Cooking: 1 hour 10 minutes

Ready In: 1 hour 50 minutes

"This is the perfect comfort food for cold days. To make it vegan, substitute non-dairy ingredients for dairy. If you want to make mashed potatoes from scratch, you will want at least 4 cups when you are through."

INGREDIENTS

1 head broccoli, cut into florets

8 ounces whole button mushrooms

3 small zucchini, chopped

2 cups chopped carrots

1/4 cup olive oil

salt and pepper to taste

3 cups water

1 cup milk

1/4 cup butter

1 (7.6 ounce) package instant mashed potato flakes

1 (12 ounce) package corn tortillas

3 cups enchilada sauce

8 ounces shredded Cheddar cheese

DIRECTIONS

1. In a large mixing bowl, combine broccoli, mushrooms, zucchini, and carrots. Drizzle the vegetables with olive oil, and season with salt and pepper. Spread vegetables in a single layer in a shallow baking dish. Roast vegetables at 425°F (220°C) for 30 to 40 minutes; stir halfway through their cooking time. When finished cooking, remove from the oven, and reduce oven temperature to 350°F (175°C).

2. Bring water, milk, and butter to a boil in a large pot. Remove the pot from heat, and mix in the mashed potato flakes. Let stand two minutes, then stir the mashed potatoes with a fork until they are smooth. Stir in roasted vegetables.

3. In a dry, nonstick skillet over medium heat, quickly heat each tortilla on both sides to make pliable. Dip the tortillas in enchilada sauce. Put a large spoonful (approximately 1/4 to 1/3 cup) of potato-veggie mixture into the center of each tortilla. Top mixture with about 1 to 2 tablespoons cheese, and roll tortillas. Place seam-side down in a 9x13 inch baking dish. Pour extra sauce over top, and sprinkle with remaining cheese.

4. Bake at 350°F (175°C) for approximately 20 to 30 minutes, or until the enchiladas are heated through.

Enchilada Casserole

Submitted by: **Carol Hilderbrand**

Makes: 8 servings

Preparation: 15 minutes

Cooking: 45 minutes

Ready In: 1 hour

"The inclusion of tempeh adds a good measure of protein to this spicy casserole. You can replace the Cheddar cheese with Monterey Jack if you like. Serve with sour cream and salsa!"

INGREDIENTS

1 (15 ounce) can black beans, rinsed and drained

2 cloves garlic, minced

1 onion, chopped

1 (4 ounce) can diced green chile peppers

1 jalapeno pepper, seeded and minced

1 (8 ounce) package tempeh, crumbled

6 (6 inch) corn tortillas

1 (19 ounce) can enchilada sauce

1 (6 ounce) can sliced black olives

8 ounces shredded Cheddar cheese

DIRECTIONS

1. Preheat oven to 350°(175°C). Lightly oil a 9x13 inch baking dish.

2. In a medium bowl, combine the beans, garlic, onion, chile peppers, jalapeno pepper, and tempeh. Pour enchilada sauce into a shallow bowl.

3. Dip three tortillas in the enchilada sauce, and place them in the prepared baking dish. Be sure to cover the bottom of the dish as completely as possible. Place ½ of the bean mixture on top of the tortillas, and repeat. Drizzle the remaining sauce over the casserole, and sprinkle with olives and shredded cheese.

4. Cover, and bake for 30 minutes. Uncover, and continue baking for an additional 15 minutes, or until the casserole is bubbling and the cheese is melted.

Seven Layer Tortilla Pie

Submitted by: **Karen C. Greenlee**

Makes: 6 servings

Preparation: 15 minutes

Cooking: 40 minutes

Ready In: 55 minutes

"Looks like a pie, cuts like a pie, and tastes like a little bit of Southwestern heaven. This casserole is made from pinto and black beans layered with tortillas and cheese. Picante sauce gives it just the right kick. You can replace the Cheddar cheese with Monterey Jack if you like."

INGREDIENTS

2 (15 ounce) cans pinto beans, drained and rinsed

1 cup salsa, divided

2 cloves garlic, minced

2 tablespoons chopped fresh cilantro

1 (15 ounce) can black beans, rinsed and drained

½ cup chopped tomatoes

7 (8 inch) flour tortillas

2 cups shredded reduced-fat Cheddar cheese

1 cup salsa

½ cup sour cream

DIRECTIONS

1. Preheat oven to 400°F (200°C).

2. In a large bowl, mash pinto beans. Stir in ¾ cup salsa and garlic.

3. In a separate bowl, mix together ¼ cup salsa, cilantro, black beans and tomatoes.

4. Place 1 tortilla in a pie plate or tart dish. Spread ¾ cup pinto bean mixture over tortilla to within ½ inch of edge. Top with ¼ cup cheese, and cover with another tortilla. Spread with ⅔ cup black bean mixture, and top with ¼ cup cheese. Repeat layering twice. Cover with remaining tortilla, and spread with remaining pinto bean mixture and cheese.

5. Cover with foil, and bake in preheated oven for about 40 minutes. Cut into wedges, and serve with salsa and sour cream.

Zesty Taco Casserole

Submitted by: **Gail & David**

Makes: 8 servings

Preparation: 20 minutes

Cooking: 40 minutes

Ready In: 1 hour

"A quick, filling, zesty vegetarian taco casserole. Yumm! Yumm!"

INGREDIENTS

1 cup uncooked white rice

2 cups water

1 tablespoon vegetable oil

1 large onion, chopped

1 large green bell pepper, chopped

1 large red bell pepper, chopped

2 cloves garlic, chopped

1 (7 ounce) can chopped green chile peppers

1 cup salsa

3 tablespoons chili powder

2 tablespoons ground cumin

1 tablespoon dried oregano

2 cups cottage cheese

1 (8.75 ounce) can whole kernel corn, drained

1 (15.25 ounce) can vegetarian chili

2 cups coarsely crushed corn chips

½ cup shredded Cheddar cheese

DIRECTIONS

1. Combine rice and water In a saucepan, and bring to a boil. Reduce heat, cover, and simmer for 20 minutes. Preheat oven to 350°F (175°C).

2. Meanwhile, heat oil in a large skillet over medium heat. Cook onion, green bell pepper, red bell pepper, and garlic in oil until tender. In a medium bowl, combine chile peppers, salsa, chili powder, cumin, oregano, cottage cheese, corn, chili, and cooked rice. Stir this mixture in with the onions and peppers. Cook until heated through. Transfer to a 2 quart casserole dish, and top with chips and cheese. Use more or less cheese to taste.

3. Bake in preheated oven for 20 minutes.

side dish

You'll find plenty of convenient solutions waiting for you in this chapter, from the summery Zucchini Casserole to the wintery Slow Cooker Stuffing, and Sweet Potato Casserole. Many of these superior accompaniments can be served at any time of the year—when you're called upon to bring a dish to an outdoor barbeque or a large family gathering.

All Day Macaroni and Cheese

Submitted by: **Becky**

Makes: 6 servings

Preparation: 15 minutes

Cooking: 6 hours 10 minutes

Ready In: 6 hours 25 minutes

"It takes all day to cook, but just a few minutes to prepare! A rich macaroni and cheese dish made with evaporated milk to make it even creamier!"

INGREDIENTS

8 ounces elbow macaroni

4 cups shredded sharp Cheddar cheese

1 (12 fluid ounce) can evaporated milk

1½ cups milk

2 eggs

1 teaspoon salt

½ teaspoon ground black pepper

DIRECTIONS

1. In a large pot, cook the macaroni in boiling water 10 minutes, or until al dente, and drain.

2. In a large bowl, mix the cooked macaroni, 3 cups of the sharp Cheddar cheese, evaporated milk, milk, eggs, salt, and pepper. Transfer to a slow cooker that has been coated with non-stick cooking spray. Sprinkle with the remaining 1 cup of shredded sharp Cheddar cheese.

3. Cover, and cook on Low for 5 to 6 hours, or until the mixture is firm and golden around the edges. Do not remove the cover or stir the mixture until the mixture has finished cooking. Serve warm.

Slow Cooker Chicken Dressing

Submitted by: **Mindy McCoy**

Makes: 16 servings

Preparation: 30 minutes

Cooking: 4 hours 30 minutes

Ready In: 5 hours

"Slow cooker dressing made with chicken breast, cornbread, chicken broth, cream of chicken soup, eggs and onion — and flavored with sage."

INGREDIENTS

5 skinless, boneless chicken breast halves

1 (9x9 inch) pan cornbread, cooled and crumbled

8 slices day-old bread, torn into small pieces

4 eggs, beaten

1 onion, chopped

1 teaspoon salt

1 teaspoon ground black pepper

2 teaspoons dried sage

2 (14.5 ounce) cans chicken broth

2 (10.75 ounce) cans condensed cream of chicken soup

2 tablespoons margarine

DIRECTIONS

1. Place chicken in a pot with water to cover, and bring to a boil over medium heat. Boil 20 minutes, or until cooked through. Cool, and cut into pieces.

2. In a slow cooker, stir together chicken, cornbread, bread, eggs, onion, salt, pepper, sage, chicken broth, and chicken soup. Stir until well blended. Dot with margarine.

3. Cover, and cook on Low for 3 to 4 hours. Remove lid, and fluff with fork. Let rest 15 minutes before serving.

Slow Cooker Stuffing

Submitted by: **Gayle Wagner**

Makes: 16 servings

Preparation: 25 minutes

Cooking: 8 hours 55 minutes

Ready In: 9 hours 20 minutes

"This is an easy way to make extra stuffing for a large crowd, saving stove space because it cooks in a slow cooker. Very tasty and moist!"

INGREDIENTS

1 cup butter

2 cups chopped onion

2 cups chopped celery

12 ounces fresh mushrooms, sliced

1/4 cup fresh parsley

12 1/2 cups dry bread cubes

1 teaspoon poultry seasoning

1 1/2 teaspoons dried sage

1 teaspoon dried thyme

1/2 teaspoon dried marjoram

1 1/2 teaspoons salt

1/2 teaspoon ground black pepper

4 1/2 cups chicken broth

2 eggs, beaten

DIRECTIONS

1. Melt butter or margarine in a skillet over medium heat. Cook onion, celery, mushroom, and parsley in butter, stirring frequently.

2. Spoon cooked vegetables over bread cubes in a very large mixing bowl. Season with poultry seasoning, sage, thyme, marjoram, and salt and pepper. Pour in enough broth to moisten, and mix in eggs. Transfer mixture to slow cooker, and cover.

3. Cook on High for 45 minutes, then reduce heat to Low, and cook for 4 to 8 hours.

Frijoles II

Submitted by: **Brandi**

Makes: 4 servings

Preparation: 15 minutes

Cooking: 6 hours

Ready In: 6 hours 15 minutes

"This recipe is similar to refried beans without the frying. These slow cooker beans will go well with any of your favorite Mexican dinners. For faster cooking, soak beans overnight."

INGREDIENTS

1½ cups dry pinto beans

½ teaspoon white sugar

1 teaspoon minced garlic

2 tablespoons finely chopped onion

2 slices smoked bacon

2 cups water

salt to taste

DIRECTIONS

1. Place the beans, sugar, garlic, onion, and bacon into a slow cooker. Pour in the water, cover, and cook on High for 6 hours. Drain off ⅔ of the liquid, and discard bacon. Use a potato masher to mash beans to a chunky consistency. Season with salt to taste, and serve hot.

Slow Cooker Creamed Corn

Submitted by: **Danielle**

Makes: 10 to 12 servings

Preparation: 10 minutes

Cooking: 4 hours

Ready In: 4 hours 10 minutes

"Good and easy!"

INGREDIENTS

1¼ (16 ounce) packages frozen corn kernels

1 (8 ounce) package cream cheese

½ cup butter

½ cup milk

1 tablespoon white sugar

salt and pepper to taste

DIRECTIONS

1. In a slow cooker, combine corn, cream cheese, butter, milk, and sugar. Season with salt and pepper to taste.

2. Cook on High for 2 to 4 hours, or on Low for 4 to 6 hours.

Slow Cooker Scalloped Potatoes with Ham

Submitted by: **Raquel Davis**

Makes: 8 servings

Preparation: 20 minutes

Cooking: 4 hours

Ready In: 4 hours 20 minutes

"If you like ham and potatoes, you'll love this creamy recipe! Its a big hit in my house, especially with my kids!"

INGREDIENTS

3 pounds potatoes, peeled and thinly sliced

1 cup shredded Cheddar cheese

½ cup chopped onion

1 cup chopped cooked ham

1 (10.75 ounce) can condensed cream of mushroom soup

½ cup water

½ teaspoon garlic powder

¼ teaspoon salt

¼ teaspoon black pepper

DIRECTIONS

1. Place sliced potatoes in slow cooker. In a medium bowl, mix together shredded cheese, onion and ham. Mix with potatoes in slow cooker. Using the same bowl, mix together condensed soup and water. Season to taste with garlic powder, salt and pepper. Pour evenly over the potato mixture.

2. Cover, and cook on High for 4 hours.

Corny Ham and Potato Scallop

Submitted by: **Mary Lee Jones**

Makes: 6 servings

Preparation: 20 minutes

Cooking: 8 hours

Ready In: 8 hours 20 minutes

"Slow cooked ham and cheesy potatoes with corn and bell pepper."

INGREDIENTS

5 potatoes, peeled and cubed

1½ cups cubed cooked ham

1 (15 ounce) can whole kernel corn, drained

¼ cup chopped green bell pepper

2 teaspoons dried minced onion

1 (10.75 ounce) can condensed Cheddar cheese soup

½ cup milk

3 tablespoons all-purpose flour

DIRECTIONS

1. In a slow cooker, combine potatoes, ham, corn, green pepper, and onion. In a small bowl, stir together soup, milk, and flour until smooth. Pour soup mixture over ham and vegetables, and stir gently to coat.

2. Cover, and cook on Low for about 8 hours, or until potatoes are tender.

Slow Cooker Green Beans, Ham and Potatoes

Submitted by: **Sharon**

Makes: 10 servings

Preparation: 30 minutes

Cooking: 4 hours

Ready In: 4 hours 30 minutes

"I make this dish often; I have never really measured the ingredients, but can give you a reasonable approximation. Note: Freeze leftover cooking liquid, and then add to bean soup, ham or cabbage dishes, or use to cook dumplings in. It's delicious!"

INGREDIENTS

2 pounds fresh green beans, rinsed and trimmed

1 large onion, chopped

3 ham hocks

1½ pounds new potatoes, quartered

1 teaspoon garlic powder

1 teaspoon onion powder

1 teaspoon seasoning salt

1 tablespoon chicken bouillon granules

ground black pepper to taste

DIRECTIONS

1. Halve beans if they are large, place in a slow cooker with water to barely cover, and add onion and ham hocks. Cover, and cook on High until simmering. Reduce heat to Low, and cook for 2 to 3 hours, or until beans are crisp but not done.

2. Add potatoes, and cook for another 45 minutes. While potatoes are cooking, remove ham hocks from slow cooker, and remove meat from bones. Chop or shred meat, and return to slow cooker. Season with garlic powder, onion powder, seasoning salt, bouillon, and pepper. Cook until potatoes are done, then adjust seasoning to taste.

3. To serve, use a slotted spoon to put beans, potatoes, and ham into a serving dish with a little broth.

Slow Cooker Mashed Potatoes

Submitted by: **Bwaye**

Makes: 8 servings

Preparation: 15 minutes

Cooking: 3 hours 15 minutes

Ready In: 3 hours 30 minutes

"These are melt in your mouth mashed potatoes, and what could be better than potatoes in the slow cooker?"

INGREDIENTS

5 pounds red potatoes, cut into chunks

1 tablespoon minced garlic, or to taste

3 cubes chicken bouillon

1 (8 ounce) container sour cream

1 (8 ounce) package cream cheese, softened

½ cup butter

salt and pepper to taste

DIRECTIONS

1. In a large pot of lightly salted boiling water, cook the potatoes, garlic, and bouillon until potatoes are tender but firm, about 15 minutes. Drain, reserving water. In a bowl, mash potatoes with sour cream and cream cheese, adding reserved water as needed to attain desired consistency.

2. Transfer the potato mixture to a slow cooker, cover, and cook on Low for 2 to 3 hours. Just before serving, stir in butter and season with salt and pepper to taste.

Party Potatoes

Submitted by: **Beth Neuenfeldt**

Makes: 8 servings

Preparation: 10 minutes

Cooking: 45 minutes

Ready In: 55 minutes

"These aren't your ordinary mashed potatoes! You can also make the mashed potatoes the day before, refrigerate overnight, then bake them the next day."

INGREDIENTS

9 large potatoes

8 ounces cream cheese

1 cup sour cream

2 teaspoons onion salt

1 teaspoon salt

1/4 teaspoon ground black pepper

2 tablespoons butter

DIRECTIONS

1. Preheat oven to 350°F (175°C). Grease a 2 quart casserole dish, and set aside.

2. Bring a large pot of lightly salted water to a boil. Cook potatoes in boiling water until tender. Drain, and transfer to a large mixing bowl. Mash until smooth. Stir in cream cheese, sour cream, onion salt, salt, and pepper. Beat until light and fluffy. Transfer to the prepared casserole dish, and dot with pieces of butter.

3. Bake for 30 minutes in the preheated oven, or until heated through.

Creamy Au Gratin Potatoes

Submitted by: **Cathy Martin**

Makes: 4 servings

Preparation: 30 minutes

Cooking: 1 hour 30 minutes

Ready In: 2 hours

"This is my husband's favorite dish, and he considers it a special occasion every time I make it. The creamy cheese sauce and the tender potatoes in this classic French dish combine to make a deliciously addictive experience. It's a great side dish with a roast pork loin or beef tenderloin. Add a green salad and French bread, and you have found the magic path to a man's heart."

INGREDIENTS

4 russet potatoes, sliced into ¼ inch slices

1 onion, sliced into rings

salt and pepper to taste

3 tablespoons butter

3 tablespoons all-purpose flour

½ teaspoon salt

2 cups milk

1½ cups shredded Cheddar cheese

DIRECTIONS

1. Preheat oven to 400°F (200°C). Butter a 1 quart casserole dish.

2. Layer ½ of the potatoes into bottom of the prepared casserole dish. Top with the onion slices, and add the remaining potatoes. Season with salt and pepper to taste.

3. In a medium-size saucepan, melt butter over medium heat. Mix in the flour and salt, and stir constantly with a whisk for one minute. Stir in milk. Cook until mixture has thickened. Stir in cheese all at once, and continue stirring until melted, about 30 to 60 seconds. Pour cheese over the potatoes, and cover the dish with aluminum foil.

4. Bake 1½ hours in the preheated oven.

Candie's Easy Potato and Onion Dish

Submitted by: **CandieAnne**

Makes: 8 servings

Preparation: 10 minutes

Cooking: 45 minutes

Ready In: 55 minutes

"If you love sweet onions with buttery potatoes, this dish is for you! Every time someone asks for the recipe they are pleased to hear how simple it is!"

INGREDIENTS

8 potatoes, sliced

2 large sweet onions, sliced

1/2 cup butter, sliced

1 tablespoon dried parsley

salt and pepper to taste

DIRECTIONS

1. Preheat oven to 350°F (175°C).

2. In a 9x13 inch casserole dish, mix the potatoes, onions, butter, and parsley. Season with salt and pepper.

3. Bake covered in the preheated oven for 45 minutes, stirring occasionally, or until potatoes are tender.

Baked Potato Salad

Submitted by: **Tom**

Makes: 12 servings

Preparation: 25 minutes

Cooking: 1 hour 20 minutes

Ready In: 1 hour 45 minutes

"Is this a baked potato salad or a cheese and potato casserole? Try this recipe and decide for yourself."

INGREDIENTS

8 medium potatoes, sliced

1/2 pound sliced bacon

1 pound processed American cheese, sliced

1/2 onion, chopped

1 cup mayonnaise

salt and pepper to taste

1/4 cup black olives, sliced

DIRECTIONS

1. Preheat oven to 325°F (165°C). Butter a 9x13 inch baking dish.

2. Put sliced potatoes into a large pot, and fill with enough water to cover. Bring to a boil, and cook until tender but still firm, about 10 minutes. Drain, and set aside.

3. At the same time, place bacon in a large deep skillet. Cook over medium-high heat until evenly browned. Remove to paper towels to drain.

4. In a large bowl, stir together the potatoes, cheese, onion, mayonnaise, salt, and pepper. Spoon into prepared baking dish. Crumble bacon over the top, and sprinkle with olives.

5. Bake for 1 hour in the preheated oven, until golden brown.

Scalloped Sweet Potatoes and Apples

Submitted by: **Linda**

Makes: 8 servings

Preparation: 15 minutes

Cooking: 1 hour 10 minutes

Ready In: 1 hour 25 minutes

"This sweet, spicy side dish is an excellent way to dress up ham or pork chops."

INGREDIENTS

6 sweet potatoes

1½ cups peeled, cored and sliced apples

½ cup brown sugar

½ teaspoon salt

1 teaspoon ground mace

¼ cup butter

DIRECTIONS

1. Place sweet potatoes in a large pot with enough water to cover, and bring to a boil. Boil until tender, then cool, peel, and cut into ¼ inch slices.

2. Preheat oven to 350°F (175°C). Grease a 9x13 inch baking dish.

3. Arrange half the sweet potatoes in the bottom of the prepared baking dish. Layer half of the apples over the sweet potatoes. In a small bowl, mix together brown sugar, salt, and mace, then sprinkle half of the mixture over the apple layer. Dot with half the butter. Repeat layers of sweet potato and apple, and top with remaining brown sugar mixture and butter.

4. Bake in the preheated oven for 50 minutes, until apples are tender and top is golden brown.

Sweet Potato Casserole II

Submitted by: **Suzanne Cook**

Makes: 16 servings

Preparation: 20 minutes

Cooking: 25 minutes

Ready In: 45 minutes

"Fluffy sweet potatoes mixed with butter, sugar, and vanilla, and baked with a crunchy pecan streusel topping. This recipe was given to me by my brother-in-law."

INGREDIENTS

4½ cups cooked and mashed sweet potatoes

½ cup butter, melted

⅓ cup milk

1 cup white sugar

½ teaspoon vanilla extract

2 eggs, beaten

1 cup light brown sugar

½ cup all-purpose flour

⅓ cup butter

1 cup chopped pecans

DIRECTIONS

1. Preheat oven to 350°F (175°C). Grease a 9x13 inch baking dish.

2. In a large bowl, mix together mashed sweet potatoes, ½ cup butter, milk, sugar, vanilla extract, and eggs. Spread sweet potato mixture into the prepared baking dish. In a small bowl, mix together brown sugar and flour. Cut in ⅓ cup butter until mixture is crumbly, then stir in pecans. Sprinkle pecan mixture over the sweet potatoes.

3. Bake for 25 minutes in the preheated oven, or until golden brown.

Asparagus Casserole

Submitted by: **KDB**

Makes: 8 servings

Preparation: 20 minutes

Cooking: 20 minutes

Ready In: 40 minutes

"This has been passed down 3 generations and is always a family favorite especially around holidays!"

INGREDIENTS

1 cup shredded Cheddar cheese

2 cups crushed saltine crackers

½ cup butter, melted

1 cup condensed cream of mushroom soup

1 (15 ounce) can asparagus, drained with liquid reserved

½ cup slivered almonds

DIRECTIONS

1. Preheat oven to 350°F (175°C).

2. In a small bowl, mix together the Cheddar cheese and cracker crumbs. In another dish, stir together the melted butter, soup, and the juice from the can of asparagus.

3. Use half of the cracker mixture to make a layer in the bottom of a 1½ quart casserole dish. Arrange half of the asparagus spears over the crumbs, sprinkle with ½ of the almonds, then pour ½ of the soup mixture over. Build another layer, starting with the remaining asparagus spears, then the remaining soup mixture, and ending with the remaining cheese and crumbs on top.

4. Bake for 20 minutes in the preheated oven, or until the top is golden.

Awesome and Easy Creamy Corn Casserole

Submitted by: **Ruthie Crickmer**

Makes: 8 servings

Preparation: 5 minutes

Cooking: 45 minutes

Ready In: 50 minutes

"This truly is the most delicious stuff! A bit like a cross between corn souffle and a slightly sweet corn pudding! Try it, I know you will love the ease of preparation and especially the taste. Everyone always wants the recipe! Note: The ingredients can be doubled and baked in a 9x13 inch baking dish in almost the same amount of cooking time."

INGREDIENTS

½ cup butter, melted

2 eggs, beaten

1 (8.5 ounce) package dry corn bread mix

1 (15 ounce) can whole kernel corn, drained

1 (14.75 ounce) can creamed corn

1 cup sour cream

DIRECTIONS

1. Preheat oven to 350°F (175°C), and lightly grease a 9x9 inch baking dish.

2. In a medium bowl, combine butter, eggs, corn bread mix, whole and creamed corn and sour cream. Spoon mixture into prepared dish.

3. Bake for 45 minutes in the preheated oven, or until the top is golden brown.

Connoisseur's Casserole

Submitted by: **April**

Makes: 8 servings

Preparation: 20 minutes

Cooking: 45 minutes

Ready In: 1 hour 5 minutes

"A great casserole that everyone will love! It freezes well."

INGREDIENTS

1 (11 ounce) can white corn, drained

1 (15 ounce) can green beans, drained

1/2 cup chopped celery

1/2 cup chopped onion

1 (2 ounce) jar chopped pimento peppers

1/2 cup sour cream

1/2 cup shredded Colby cheese

1 (10.75 ounce) can condensed cream of celery soup

1/2 teaspoon salt

1/2 teaspoon pepper

4 tablespoons butter

1/2 cup slivered almonds

1 cup crushed buttery round crackers

DIRECTIONS

1. Preheat oven to 350°F (175°C).

2. In a medium bowl, mix white corn, green beans, celery, onion, pimento peppers, sour cream, Colby cheese, cream of celery soup, salt, and pepper. Transfer to a 1½ quart casserole dish.

3. Melt butter in a small saucepan over medium heat, and stir in slivered almonds and crushed crackers. Sprinkle over the casserole.

4. Bake for 45 minutes in the preheated oven, or until bubbly and lightly browned.

Tim's Green Bean Casserole Extraordinaire

Submitted by: **Tim Pipher**

Makes: 12 servings

Preparation: 20 minutes

Cooking: 1 hour

Ready In: 1 hour 20 minutes

"Green bean casserole unlike any other!"

INGREDIENTS

¼ cup butter

¼ cup all-purpose flour

2 cups sour cream

2 cups shredded Swiss cheese

4 (14.5 ounce) cans French-style green beans, drained

2 cups cornflakes cereal, crushed

¼ cup butter, melted

DIRECTIONS

1. Preheat oven to 350°F (175°C). Grease a 1½ quart casserole dish.

2. Melt ¼ cup of butter in a large skillet. Stir flour into the butter to make a paste. Blend sour cream into the flour paste, stirring constantly. When the mixture is hot and bubbly, remove from heat, and stir in Swiss cheese. When the cheese has melted, add the green beans, stirring until they are coated. Pour the entire mixture into the prepared casserole dish.

3. In a small bowl, mix together the cornflakes and melted butter. Sprinkle over the top of the green beans.

4. Bake uncovered for 30 minutes in the preheated oven, or until bubbly and golden brown.

Squash and Apple Bake

Submitted by: **Paula**

Makes: 8 servings

Preparation: 20 minutes

Cooking: 1 hour

Ready In: 1 hour 20 minutes

"This is a recipe that combines all the best flavors of fall! Great for a Thanksgiving dinner instead of candied yams."

INGREDIENTS

½ cup packed light brown sugar

¼ cup butter, melted

1 tablespoon all-purpose flour

1 teaspoon salt

½ teaspoon ground mace

2 pounds butternut squash - peeled, seeded, and cut into ½ inch slices

2 large apples - cored, and cut into ½ inch slices

DIRECTIONS

1. Preheat oven to 350°F (175°C).

2. In a medium bowl, stir together brown sugar, butter, flour, salt, and mace. Arrange squash in an ungreased 9x13 inch baking dish. Top with slices of apple, then sprinkle with the sugar mixture. Cover with a lid or aluminum foil.

3. Bake for 50 to 60 minutes in the preheated oven, or until squash is tender.

Zucchini Casserole

Submitted by: **Maria**

Makes: 8 servings

Preparation: 30 minutes

Cooking: 45 minutes

Ready In: 1 hour 15 minutes

"This is a creative, unusual casserole that's one of my grandmother's favorites. It combines zucchini and bell pepper with Cheddar cheese, spices and crispy corn flakes. Bread crumbs can be used in place of cornflakes."

INGREDIENTS

8 cups diced zucchini

1 red bell pepper, chopped

1 cup cornflakes cereal

1 cup shredded Cheddar cheese

½ cup olive oil

1 teaspoon dried basil

2 eggs, beaten

salt and pepper to taste

DIRECTIONS

1. Preheat oven to 350°F (175°C). Lightly oil a 9x13 inch baking dish.

2. In a large bowl, combine zucchini, bell pepper, cornflakes, cheese, oil, basil, and eggs. Season with salt and pepper to taste. Spread evenly into prepared baking dish.

3. Bake in the preheated oven for 45 minutes, or until top is golden brown.

Baked Tomatoes Oregano

Submitted by: **Michele O'Sullivan**

Makes: 4 servings

Preparation: 15 minutes

Cooking: 20 minutes

Ready In: 35 minutes

"An excellent side dish. Tastes like pizza without the crust!"

INGREDIENTS

4 large ripe tomatoes, sliced 1/4 inch thick

1/8 cup grated Romano cheese

1/2 cup fresh bread crumbs

1 clove garlic, minced

2 sprigs fresh parsley, chopped

salt and pepper to taste

1/2 teaspoon dried oregano

1 tablespoon olive oil

DIRECTIONS

1. Preheat oven to 400°F (200°C). Coat a shallow baking dish with cooking spray.

2. Place tomato slices close together in prepared baking dish. Sprinkle with cheese, bread crumbs, garlic, parsley, salt, pepper, and oregano. Drizzle with olive oil.

3. Bake for 20 minutes in the preheated oven, or until cheese is lightly toasted.

Carrot Casserole

Submitted by: **Paula**

Makes: 6 servings

Preparation: 20 minutes

Cooking: 30 minutes

Ready In: 50 minutes

"Carrots, spiced sweetly! This recipe is a little heavier than a souffle, but equally as scrumptious and rich!"

INGREDIENTS

2¹/2 cups sliced carrots

1 tablespoon butter

3 eggs

1 cup white sugar

¹/3 cup milk

¹/2 teaspoon salt

1 teaspoon ground cinnamon

1 teaspoon ground nutmeg

1 teaspoon vanilla extract

DIRECTIONS

1. Preheat oven to 325°F (165°C). Grease a 1 quart casserole dish.

2. Place carrots and enough water to cover them in a small saucepan. Bring to a boil, and cook until carrots are very tender. Drain. Using a blender or food processor, puree carrots to a smooth consistency.

3. In a medium bowl, mix together the carrots and butter. Beat in the eggs, sugar, milk, salt, cinnamon, nutmeg, and vanilla. Spread mixture into the prepared casserole dish.

4. Bake for 25 to 30 minutes in the preheated oven, or until set.

Cauliflower Casserole

Submitted by: **Betty Houston**

Makes: 6 servings

Preparation: 15 minutes

Cooking: 30 minutes

Ready In: 45 minutes

"A quick, delightful dish that is easy to make and sure to please! Those who say they hate cauliflower always enjoy this dish."

INGREDIENTS

1 large head cauliflower, broken into small florets

½ cup butter, melted

¼ cup grated Parmesan cheese

⅔ cup Italian seasoned bread crumbs

1 pinch salt

1 teaspoon crushed red pepper flakes

1 cup shredded Cheddar cheese

DIRECTIONS

1. Preheat oven to 350°F (175°C).

2. Bring 2 inches of water to a boil in a medium saucepan. Add cauliflower, cover, and cook for about 10 minutes. Drain, and place in a 2 quart casserole dish.

3. In a small bowl mix together butter, Parmesan cheese, bread crumbs, salt, and red pepper flakes. Sprinkle mixture over cauliflower, and top with Cheddar cheese.

4. Bake in the preheated oven for 20 minutes, or until cheese is melted and bubbly.

Aunt Millie's Broccoli Casserole

Submitted by: **Kaylee**

Makes: 10 servings

Preparation: 15 minutes

Cooking: 40 minutes

Ready In: 55 minutes

"This is a family favorite for holidays and get-togethers! This recipe has been passed down in our family for years because it's so cheesy and delicious!"

INGREDIENTS

4 heads fresh broccoli, chopped

1½ cups shredded American cheese

1 (10.75 ounce) can condensed cream of mushroom soup

1½ teaspoons salt

2 teaspoons ground black pepper

3 tablespoons butter

2 cups crushed, seasoned croutons

DIRECTIONS

1. Preheat oven to 350°F (175°C).

2. Bring a pot of lightly salted water to a boil. Cook broccoli in the boiling water for 1 minute. Drain, and set aside.

3. In a saucepan over medium heat, mix the cheese, cream of mushroom soup, salt, and pepper. Stir until cheese is melted. Add the broccoli, stirring to coat. Transfer the mixture to a 9x13 inch baking dish.

4. In a separate saucepan, melt the butter over medium heat. Mix in the croutons, and sprinkle over the broccoli mixture.

5. Bake 30 minutes in the preheated oven, until the topping is browned and broccoli is tender.

Beth's Scalloped Cabbage

Submitted by: **Beth Leslie**

Makes: 6 servings

Preparation: 10 minutes

Cooking: 40 minutes

Ready In: 50 minutes

"Excellent holiday side dish."

INGREDIENTS

1 medium head cabbage, cut into small wedges

2 tablespoons butter

2 tablespoons all-purpose flour

1/2 teaspoon salt

1 cup milk

2/3 cup shredded American cheese

1/2 cup crushed buttery round crackers

DIRECTIONS

1. Preheat oven to 350°F (175°C). Grease a 2 quart casserole dish.

2. Bring a large pot of salted water to a boil. Cook cabbage in boiling water until barely tender, about 10 minutes; drain.

3. Meanwhile, melt butter in a small saucepan over low heat. Blend in flour, milk, and salt. Cook and stir until slightly thickened, and then fold in cheese.

4. Transfer cabbage to prepared casserole dish, and stir in cheese sauce. Sprinkle cracker crumbs on top.

5. Bake for 25 to 30 minutes in the preheated oven, or until top is browned.

Mouse's Macaroni and Cheese

Submitted by: **Mouse**

Makes: 6 servings

Preparation: 15 minutes

Cooking: 35 minutes

Ready In: 50 minutes

"The cheesiest and easiest recipe I know."

INGREDIENTS

1½ cups uncooked elbow macaroni

¼ cup butter

2 tablespoons all-purpose flour

1 teaspoon mustard powder

1 teaspoon ground black pepper

2 cups milk

8 ounces American cheese, cubed

8 ounces processed cheese food (e.g. Velveeta), cubed

¼ cup seasoned dry bread crumbs

DIRECTIONS

1. Preheat oven to 400°F (205°C). Butter a 1½ quart casserole dish. Bring a saucepan of lightly salted water to a boil. Add macaroni, and cook until not quite done, about 6 minutes. Drain.

2. In a separate saucepan, melt the butter over medium heat. Blend in the flour, mustard powder, and pepper until smooth. Slowly stir in the milk, beating out any lumps. Add the American and processed cheeses, and stir constantly until the sauce is thick and smooth.

3. Drain noodles, and stir them into the cheese sauce. Transfer the mixture to the prepared casserole dish. Sprinkle bread crumbs over the top.

4. Cover the dish, and bake for 20 to 25 minutes, or until sauce is thick and bubbly.

Baked Mushroom Rice

Submitted by: **Maryanne**

Makes: 6 servings

Preparation: 15 minutes

Cooking: 40 minutes

Ready In: 55 minutes

"You can vary this easy rice side dish by adding different spices or meat."

INGREDIENTS

2 cups uncooked white rice

1 (10.75 ounce) can condensed cream of mushroom soup

1 cup vegetable broth

1/2 cup chopped onion

1/4 cup fresh chopped mushrooms

1 teaspoon dried parsley

1 teaspoon dried oregano

1/4 cup butter, melted

salt and pepper to taste

DIRECTIONS

1. Preheat oven to 400°F (200°C).

2. In a large bowl, stir together the white rice, cream of mushroom soup, and vegetable broth. Blend in the onion, mushrooms, parsley, oregano, melted butter, salt, and pepper. Transfer to a 2 quart baking dish, and cover with a lid or aluminum foil.

3. Bake for 35 to 40 minutes in the preheated oven. If the rice is looking dry before it is tender, then pour in a little water and continue cooking until rice is tender.

Green Rice

Submitted by: **Andrea**

Makes: 6 servings

Preparation: 10 minutes

Cooking: 50 minutes

Ready In: 1 hour

"Excellent way to sneak in veggies. Use fresh or frozen spinach. Also good with one package of chopped broccoli instead of the spinach."

INGREDIENTS

2½ cups water

1¼ cups uncooked white rice

1 (10 ounce) package spinach, chopped

1 egg

1 (12 fluid ounce) can evaporated milk

1 cup shredded Cheddar cheese

DIRECTIONS

1. Preheat oven to 350°F (175°C). Lightly oil a 2 quart casserole dish.

2. In a saucepan, combine water and rice, and bring to a boil. Reduce heat, cover, and simmer for 20 minutes. Remove from heat, and stir in the spinach, egg, evaporated milk, and cheese. Spoon into the prepared casserole dish.

3. Bake for 30 minutes in the preheated oven, or until middle is set.

Barley Bake

Submitted by: **Kat**

Makes: 6 servings

Preparation: 15 minutes

Cooking: 1 hour 25 minutes

Ready In: 1 hour 40 minutes

"Easy and good dish for potlucks. The pine nuts make all the difference! The mushrooms are optional. Garnish with fresh parsley."

INGREDIENTS

¼ cup butter

1 medium onion, diced

1 cup uncooked pearl barley

½ cup pine nuts

2 green onions, thinly sliced

½ cup sliced fresh mushrooms

½ cup chopped fresh parsley

¼ teaspoon salt

⅛ teaspoon pepper

2 (14.5 ounce) cans vegetable broth

DIRECTIONS

1. Preheat oven to 350°F (175°C).

2. Melt butter in a skillet over medium-high heat. Stir in onion, barley, and pine nuts. Cook and stir until barley is lightly browned. Mix in green onions, mushrooms, and parsley. Season with salt and pepper. Transfer the mixture to a 2 quart casserole dish, and stir in the vegetable broth.

3. Bake 1 hour and 15 minutes in the preheated oven, or until liquid has been absorbed and barley is tender.

Zesty Hominy and Cheese

Submitted by: **Jeanie Bean**

Makes: 6 servings

Preparation: 5 minutes

Cooking: 25 minutes

Ready In: 30 minutes

"A different sidedish using hominy, sour cream, cheese and green chilies. Friends who say they don't like hominy eat it and ask for more. It's fast and tasty. Adjust chili peppers to taste."

INGREDIENTS

3 (15 ounce) cans white hominy, drained

1 (8 ounce) container sour cream

2 cups shredded Cheddar cheese

1 (4 ounce) can chopped green chile peppers

1 pinch cayenne pepper (optional)

DIRECTIONS

1. Preheat oven to 350°F (175°C).

2. In a 2 quart casserole dish, mix together hominy, sour cream, cheddar cheese, chilies and cayenne pepper.

3. Bake for 25 minutes in the preheated oven, or until heated through.

Boston Baked Beans

Submitted by: **Anita Rhodes**

Makes: 6 servings

Preparation: 30 minutes

Cooking: 6 hours

Ready In: 14 hours 30 minutes

"A wonderful old-fashioned baked bean flavor. This recipe has been served by my family for 29 years and originally came from my mother-in-law. It tastes great served with fresh cornbread or biscuits and honey. Although you need to allow time for soaking and simmering the beans, this recipe is still quite easy."

INGREDIENTS

2 cups navy beans

1/2 pound bacon

1 onion, finely diced

3 tablespoons molasses

2 teaspoons salt

1/4 teaspoon ground black pepper

1/4 teaspoon dry mustard

1/2 cup ketchup

1 tablespoon Worcestershire sauce

1/4 cup brown sugar

DIRECTIONS

1. Soak beans overnight in cold water. Simmer the beans in the same water until tender, approximately 1 to 2 hours. Drain and reserve the liquid.

2. Preheat oven to 325°F (165°C).

3. Arrange the beans in a 2 quart bean pot or casserole dish by placing a portion of the beans in the bottom of dish, and layering them with bacon and onion.

4. In a saucepan, combine molasses, salt, pepper, dry mustard, ketchup, Worcestershire sauce and brown sugar. Bring the mixture to a boil and pour over beans. Pour in just enough of the reserved bean water to cover the beans. Cover the dish with a lid or aluminum foil.

5. Bake for 3 to 4 hours in the preheated oven, until beans are tender. Remove the lid about halfway through cooking, and add more liquid if necessary to prevent the beans from getting too dry.

brunch

Cheesy grits, fancy frittatas, sausage-filled stratas, and hearty hash brown casseroles are the perfect way to get everyone's day off to a savory start. Having all your favorite breakfast foods in one dish is both convenient and tasty; what's more, you can prepare many of these dishes the night before.

Kielbasa and Potato Bake

Submitted by: **Geneva**

Makes: 8 servings

Preparation: 15 minutes

Cooking: 1 hour 30 minutes

Ready In: 1 hour 45 minutes

"An easy variation of the now classic brunch potato bake that includes a very tender Kielbasa."

INGREDIENTS

1 (10.75 ounce) can condensed cream of mushroom soup

2 cups milk

1 tablespoon minced garlic

1 teaspoon salt

½ teaspoon ground black pepper

1 pound kielbasa sausage, sliced thin

4 large russet potatoes, peeled and cubed

DIRECTIONS

1. Preheat oven to 375 °F (190°C).

2. In a large mixing bowl, mix together soup, milk, garlic, salt, and pepper. Stir in potatoes and kielbasa. Spoon into a 7x11 inch casserole dish.

3. Place casserole on a baking sheet, and bake in the preheated oven for 90 minutes, or until potatoes are tender.

Bangers and Mash

Submitted by: **Amanda Fair**

Makes: 8 servings
Preparation: 15 minutes
Cooking: 45 minutes
Ready In: 1 hour

"A great British dish my grandmother made for us on those cold and stormy days."

INGREDIENTS

8 large baking potatoes, peeled and quartered

2 teaspoons butter, divided

1/2 cup milk, or as needed

salt and pepper to taste

1 1/2 pounds beef sausage

1/2 cup diced onion

1 (.75 ounce) package dry brown gravy mix

1 cup water, or as needed

DIRECTIONS

1. Preheat the oven to 350°F (175°C). Place potatoes in a saucepan with enough water to cover. Bring to a boil, and cook until tender, about 20 minutes. Drain, and mash with 1 teaspoon of butter, and enough milk to reach your desired creaminess. Continue mashing, or beat with an electric mixer, until smooth. Season with salt and pepper.

2. In a large skillet over medium heat, cook the sausage until heated through. Remove from pan, and set aside. Add remaining teaspoon of butter to the skillet, and fry the onions over medium heat until tender. Mix gravy mix and water as directed on the package, and add to the skillet with the onions. Simmer, stirring constantly, to form a thick gravy.

3. Pour half of the gravy into a square casserole dish so that it coats the bottom. Place sausages in a layer over the gravy (you can butterfly the sausages if you wish). Pour remaining gravy over them, then top with mashed potatoes.

4. Bake uncovered for 20 minutes in the preheated oven, or until potatoes are evenly brown.

Sausage Casserole

Submitted by: **Bill Rossbach**

Makes: 12 servings

Preparation: 25 minutes

Cooking: 1 hour 15 minutes

Ready In: 1 hour 45 minutes

"Mouth watering, bowl scraping good! This recipe also makes a great dinner entree!"

INGREDIENTS

1 pound sage flavored breakfast sausage

3 cups shredded potatoes, drained and pressed

¼ cup butter, melted

12 ounces mild Cheddar cheese, shredded

½ cup onion, shredded

1 (16 ounce) container small curd cottage cheese

6 jumbo eggs

DIRECTIONS

1. Preheat oven to 375°F (190°C). Lightly grease a 9x13 inch square baking dish.

2. Place sausage in a large, deep skillet. Cook over medium-high heat until evenly brown. Drain, crumble, and set aside.

3. In the prepared baking dish, stir together the shredded potatoes and butter. Line the bottom and sides of the baking dish with the mixture. In a bowl, mix the sausage, Cheddar cheese, onion, cottage cheese, and eggs. Pour over the potato mixture.

4. Bake 1 hour in the preheated oven, or until a toothpick inserted into center of the casserole comes out clean. Let cool for 5 minutes before serving.

Breakfast Casserole II

Submitted by: **Sue Schuler**

Makes: 12 servings

Preparation: 15 minutes

Cooking: 1 hour

Ready In: 1 hour 15 minutes

"A great holiday breakfast casserole that may be made the night before, and baked while opening Christmas presents."

INGREDIENTS

1 (16 ounce) package ground pork breakfast sausage

12 eggs

1 (10.75 ounce) can condensed cream of mushroom soup

1 ¼ cups milk

1 (4.5 ounce) can sliced mushrooms, drained

1 (32 ounce) package frozen potato rounds

½ cup shredded Cheddar cheese

DIRECTIONS

1. Place sausage in a skillet over medium-high heat, and cook until evenly brown. Drain, and set aside.

2. Preheat oven to 350°F (175°C). Lightly grease a 9x13 inch baking dish.

3. In a large bowl, beat together the eggs, condensed cream of mushroom soup, and milk. Stir in the sausage and mushrooms, and pour into the prepared baking dish. Mix in the frozen potato rounds.

4. Bake in preheated oven for 45 to 50 minutes. Sprinkle with cheese, and bake an additional 10 minutes, or until cheese is melted.

Cheesy Ham and Hash Brown Casserole

Submitted by: **Melissa Wardell**

Makes: 12 servings

Preparation: 15 minutes

Cooking: 1 hour

Ready In: 1 hour 15 minutes

"I mostly use this as a breakfast casserole, but it's great anytime. May be served with or without diced ham. Quick and easy to make, not to mention delicious!"

INGREDIENTS

1 (32 ounce) package frozen hash brown potatoes

8 ounces cooked, diced ham

2 (10.75 ounce) cans condensed cream of potato soup

1 (16 ounce) container sour cream

2 cups shredded sharp Cheddar cheese

1½ cups grated Parmesan cheese

DIRECTIONS

1. Preheat oven to 375°F (190°C). Lightly grease a 9x13 inch baking dish.

2. In a large bowl, mix hash browns, ham, cream of potato soup, sour cream, and Cheddar cheese. Spread evenly into prepared dish. Sprinkle with Parmesan cheese.

3. Bake 1 hour in the preheated oven, or until bubbly and lightly brown. Serve immediately.

Farmer's Casserole

Submitted by: **Lorrie Starks**

Makes: 6 servings

Preparation: 25 minutes

Cooking: 45 minutes

Ready In: 1 hour 10 minutes

"Layer the ingredients in a baking dish the night before, then cover and refrigerate. In the morning, pop the casserole into the oven about an hour before serving. Serve with melon wedges, fresh strawberries, and orange wedges."

INGREDIENTS

3 cups frozen hash brown potatoes

3/4 cup shredded pepperjack cheese

1 cup cooked ham, diced

1/4 cup chopped green onions

4 eggs, beaten

1 (12 fluid ounce) can evaporated milk

1/4 teaspoon ground black pepper

1/8 teaspoon salt

DIRECTIONS

1. Preheat oven to 350°F (175°C). Grease a 2 quart baking dish.

2. Arrange hash brown potatoes evenly in the bottom of the prepared dish. Sprinkle with pepperjack cheese, ham, and green onions.

3. In a medium bowl, mix the eggs, evaporated milk, pepper, and salt. Pour the egg mixture over the potato mixture in the dish. The dish may be covered and refrigerated at this point for several hours or overnight.

4. Bake for 40 to 45 minutes (or 55 to 60 minutes if made ahead and chilled) in the preheated oven, or until a knife inserted in the center comes out clean. Let stand 5 minutes before serving.

Egg and Hash Brown Pie

Submitted by: **Ann M. Hester**

Makes: 8 servings

Preparation: 15 minutes

Cooking: 45 minutes

Ready In: 1 hour 5 minutes

"Not only is this casserole easy to make and great tasting, its pleasing to the eyes with its shades of golden brown, yellow, and green. This dish is great served with sliced fruit and toast or muffins. You may substitute chopped cooked ham for the bacon if you wish."

INGREDIENTS

6 slices bacon

5 eggs

1/2 cup milk

3 cups frozen hash brown potatoes, thawed

1/3 cup chopped green onions

1 1/2 cups shredded Cheddar cheese, divided

DIRECTIONS

1. Place bacon in a large, deep skillet. Cook over medium-high heat until evenly brown. Drain, crumble, and set aside.

2. Preheat oven to 350°F (175°C). Lightly grease a 7x11 inch baking dish.

3. In a large bowl, beat together the eggs and milk. Stir in the bacon, hash browns, green onions, and 1 cup shredded Cheddar cheese. Pour into the prepared baking dish.

4. Bake in the preheated oven 25 to 35 minutes, or until a knife inserted in the center comes out clean. Sprinkle the remaining Cheddar cheese on top, and continue baking for 3 to 4 minutes, or until the cheese is melted. Remove from oven, and let sit 5 minutes before serving.

Bagel and Cheese Bake

Submitted by: **Muse**

Makes: 12 servings

Preparation: 30 minutes

Cooking: 30 minutes

Ready In: 9 hours

"This recipe is made the night before and popped in the oven in the morning. A great homemade breakfast sandwich taste in a casserole form."

INGREDIENTS

½ pound bacon, diced

½ cup chopped onion

3 plain bagels, halved

1 cup shredded sharp Cheddar cheese

12 eggs, beaten

2 cups milk

2 teaspoons chopped fresh parsley

¼ teaspoon pepper

½ cup grated Parmesan cheese

DIRECTIONS

1. Place the bacon and onion in a large, deep skillet. Cook over medium-high heat until evenly brown. Drain, and set aside.

2. Arrange 6 bagel halves in the bottom of a lightly greased 9x13 inch baking dish. Cover with the bacon and onion mixture, followed by the Cheddar cheese. Top with remaining bagel slices.

3. In a medium bowl, whisk together the eggs, milk, parsley, and pepper. Pour the egg mixture over the bagel layers. Cover, and refrigerate 8 hours or overnight.

4. Preheat oven to 400°F (200°C). Uncover the chilled bagel dish, and bake in the preheated oven 25 to 30 minutes, or until eggs are firm. Sprinkle with Parmesan cheese, and serve warm.

Sausage Egg Casserole

Submitted by: **Linda McCann**

Makes: 12 servings

Preparation: 20 minutes

Cooking: 1 hour 20 minutes

Ready In: 9 hours 40 minutes

"Assemble the ingredients the night before, and bake this casserole in the morning. Stand back and wait for the compliments. I've made it with fat free cottage cheese, egg substitute, and reduced fat sausage; the taste is still wonderful!"

INGREDIENTS

¾ pound ground pork sausage

1 tablespoon butter

4 green onions, chopped

½ pound fresh mushrooms, sliced

10 eggs, beaten

1 (16 ounce) container low-fat cottage cheese

1 pound Monterey Jack cheese, shredded

2 (4 ounce) cans diced green chile peppers, drained

1 cup all-purpose flour

1 teaspoon baking powder

½ teaspoon salt

⅓ cup butter, melted

DIRECTIONS

1. Place sausage in a large, deep skillet. Cook over medium-high heat until evenly brown. Drain, and set aside. Melt butter in skillet, and cook and stir the green onions and mushrooms until tender.

2. In a large bowl, mix the eggs, cottage cheese, Monterey Jack cheese, and chiles. Stir in the sausage, green onions, and mushrooms. Cover, and refrigerate overnight.

3. Preheat oven to 350°F (175°C). Lightly grease a 9x13 inch baking dish.

4. In a bowl, sift together the flour, baking powder, and salt. Blend in the melted butter. Stir the flour mixture into the egg mixture. Pour into the prepared baking dish.

5. Bake 40 to 50 minutes in the preheated oven, or until lightly brown. Let stand 10 minutes before serving.

Egg and Sausage Casserole

Submitted by: **LeAnn**

Makes: 12 servings

Preparation: 15 minutes

Cooking: 35 minutes

Ready In: 50 minutes

"This recipe was given to me by a friend several years ago. It's easy to make and always a hit! Co-workers beg for it, and it's my husband's favorite!"

INGREDIENTS

1 pound pork sausage

1 (8 ounce) package refrigerated crescent roll dough

8 eggs, beaten

2 cups shredded mozzarella cheese

2 cups shredded Cheddar cheese

1 teaspoon dried oregano

DIRECTIONS

1. Place sausage in a large, deep skillet. Cook over medium-high heat until evenly brown. Drain, crumble, and set aside.

2. Preheat oven to 325°F (165°C). Lightly grease a 9x13 inch baking dish.

3. Line the bottom of the prepared baking dish with crescent roll dough, and sprinkle with crumbled sausage. In a large bowl, mix beaten eggs, mozzarella, and Cheddar. Season the mixture with oregano, and pour over the sausage and crescent rolls.

4. Bake 25 to 30 minutes in the preheated oven, or until a knife inserted in the center comes out clean.

Easy Sausage Strata

Submitted by: **Lisa Rosenkrans**

Makes: 8 servings

Preparation: 20 minutes

Cooking: 1 hour 10 minutes

Ready In: 10 hours

"This strata is really easy to make. Put it together the day before, then just remove from the refrigerator and bake. Ham or bacon can be substituted for the sausage. Sometimes I add cooked chopped broccoli for a change of pace."

INGREDIENTS

1 pound pork sausage

6 (1 ounce) slices bread, cubed

2 cups shredded Cheddar cheese

6 eggs

2 cups milk

1 teaspoon salt

1 teaspoon ground dry mustard

DIRECTIONS

1. Place sausage in a large, deep skillet. Cook over medium-high heat until evenly brown. Drain, and set aside.

2. Layer bread cubes, sausage, and Cheddar cheese in a lightly greased 7x11 inch baking dish. In a bowl, beat together the eggs, milk, salt, and mustard. Pour the egg mixture over the bread cube mixture. Cover, and refrigerate at least 8 hours or overnight.

3. Remove the casserole from the refrigerator 30 minutes before baking. Preheat oven to 350°F (175°C).

4. Bake 50 to 60 minutes in the preheated oven, or until a knife inserted in the center comes out clean. Let stand 10 minutes before serving.

Zippy Egg Casserole

Submitted by: **Susan Madsen**

Makes: 12 servings

Preparation: 15 minutes

Cooking: 1 hour 10 minutes

Ready In: 9 hours 45 minutes

"This egg casserole has a little zip to it due to the pepperjack cheese! A big hit at church brunches."

INGREDIENTS

1 pound pork sausage

1 (5.5 ounce) package seasoned croutons

1½ cups shredded Cheddar cheese

1 cup shredded Swiss cheese

1 cup shredded pepperjack cheese

8 eggs

1 pint half-and-half cream

1½ cups milk

1½ teaspoons dry mustard

1 tablespoon minced onion

salt and pepper to taste

DIRECTIONS

1. Place sausage in a large, deep skillet. Cook over medium-high heat until evenly brown. Drain, crumble, and set aside.

2. In a lightly greased 9x13 inch baking dish, arrange the croutons in a single layer. Layer with Cheddar cheese, Swiss cheese, and pepperjack cheese. Top with the cooked sausage.

3. In a large bowl, beat together the eggs, half-and-half, milk, mustard, onion, salt, and pepper. Pour into the dish over the sausage. Cover, and refrigerate overnight.

4. The next morning, bake in an oven preheated to 350°F (175°C) for 45 to 60 minutes. Let sit for 20 minutes before serving.

Mom's Breakfast Strata

Submitted by: **Amy Barry**

Makes: 8 servings

Preparation: 20 minutes

Cooking: 50 minutes

Ready In: 13 hours 10 minutes

"This strata makes breakfast less hectic because all the prep work is done the night before. The quantities of mushrooms, onions, and green peppers can be varied to suit the tastes of those who will be eating this dish."

INGREDIENTS

9 slices bread, torn into bite size pieces

1/2 cup diced fresh mushrooms

1/2 cup chopped green bell pepper

16 ounces Cheddar cheese, shredded

1/2 cup chopped onion

2 cups cubed cooked ham

8 eggs

2 cups milk

DIRECTIONS

1. Grease a 9x13 inch baking dish. Layer half of the torn bread in the bottom of the dish. Sprinkle the mushrooms and green bell pepper evenly over the bread layer. Sprinkle with half of the cheese. Top with remaining bread pieces, then layer with the onion and ham. Sprinkle with remaining cheese. Whisk together eggs and milk; pour over the entire pan. Cover with aluminum foil, and refrigerate for 12 to 24 hours.

2. Preheat the oven to 350°F (175°C).

3. Bake covered for 35 minutes, then remove foil and bake for an additional 15 minutes, or until top is evenly brown.

Ham and Cheese Breakfast Casserole

Submitted by: **Kelly**

Makes: 12 servings

Preparation: 30 minutes

Cooking: 40 minutes

Ready In: 9 hours 15 minutes

"This ham and cheese casserole is very filling. It should be assembled and then refrigerated overnight. I usually make this Christmas Eve and serve it Christmas morning after we open our presents."

INGREDIENTS

18 (1 ounce) slices white bread, cubed

8 ounces cooked ham, cubed

2 cups shredded Cheddar cheese

1½ cups diced Swiss cheese

6 eggs

3½ cups milk

½ teaspoon onion powder

2 cups crushed cornflakes cereal

½ cup butter, melted

DIRECTIONS

1. Lightly grease a 9x13 inch baking dish. Line the bottom of the dish with half the bread cubes. Sprinkle with ham, Cheddar cheese, and Swiss cheese, and top with remaining bread. In a bowl, beat together the eggs, milk, and onion powder. Pour evenly over bread. Cover, and refrigerate overnight.

2. Preheat oven to 375 °F (190°C). In a small bowl, blend the crushed cornflakes and melted butter. Spread evenly over the casserole.

3. Bake 40 minutes in the preheated oven, or until bubbly and golden brown. Let stand 5 minutes before serving.

Cheesy Ham and Asparagus Bake

Submitted by: **Bettina Bryant**

Makes: 12 servings

Preparation: 25 minutes

Cooking: 25 minutes

Ready In: 1 hour

"Even if you think you don't like asparagus you have to try this. It is a wonderfully easy quiche-like casserole to throw together for breakfast. This can be prepared the night before, covered, and put in the refrigerator overnight. Just be sure to allow extra cook time."

INGREDIENTS

1½ cups chopped cooked ham

½ cup chopped onion

¼ cup chopped red bell peppers

1 (10 ounce) package frozen cut asparagus, thawed

8 eggs

2 cups milk

1 cup all-purpose flour

¼ cup grated Parmesan cheese

¾ teaspoon dried tarragon

¾ teaspoon salt

½ teaspoon black pepper

1 cup shredded Cheddar cheese

DIRECTIONS

1. Preheat oven to 425°F (220°C). Lightly grease a 9x13 inch baking dish.

2. Mix the ham, onion, red bell peppers, and asparagus in the prepared baking dish. In a large bowl, beat together the eggs, milk, flour, Parmesan, tarragon, salt, and pepper. Pour over the ham mixture.

3. Bake 20 minutes in the preheated oven, or until a knife inserted in the center comes out clean. Sprinkle with Cheddar cheese. Continue baking 3 to 5 minutes, or until cheese is melted. Let stand 5 to 10 minutes before serving.

Green Chile Frittata

Submitted by: **Melanie**

Makes: 10 servings

Preparation: 15 minutes

Cooking: 55 minutes

Ready In: 1 hour 10 minutes

"This rich recipe is great for either a brunch or breakfast. You can make this a day ahead if you want to serve it for an early morning breakfast. Just reheat in the microwave. You may use any combination of cheese in this recipe, even non-fat."

INGREDIENTS

10 eggs, beaten

½ cup all-purpose flour

1 teaspoon baking powder

1 pinch salt

1 (7 ounce) can diced green chile peppers, drained

1 (16 ounce) container low-fat cottage cheese

1 cup shredded Cheddar cheese

¼ cup melted butter

DIRECTIONS

1. Preheat oven to 400°F (200°C). Lightly grease a 9x13 inch baking dish.

2. In a large bowl, mix the eggs, flour, baking powder, and salt. Stir in the green chile peppers, cottage cheese, Cheddar cheese, and melted butter. Pour into the prepared baking dish.

3. Bake 15 minutes in the preheated oven. Reduce heat to 325°F (165°C), and continue baking for 35 to 40 minutes. Cool slightly, and cut into small squares.

Fiesta Frittata Casserole

Submitted by: **Roxanne E. Chan**

Makes: 12 servings

Preparation: 15 minutes

Cooking: 30 minutes

Ready In: 45 minutes

"Quick and easy, this casserole is the perfect summer dish. Cheese, diced chile peppers, green onion, fresh parsley, corn, and other tasty ingredients are whisked into eggs and baked. This veggie treat is great for picnics, parties, and other summertime gatherings. You can cut the cooked casserole into small squares and serve with toothpicks and salsa for dipping."

INGREDIENTS

8 eggs

2 cups sour cream

1 cup shredded Cheddar cheese

1 (4 ounce) can diced green chile peppers, drained

1 green onion, minced

1/4 cup chopped fresh parsley

1 cup frozen corn kernels

1 (15 ounce) can black beans, rinsed and drained

1/4 cup chopped red pepper

1/4 cup bacon bits

1 cup fresh salsa

DIRECTIONS

1. Preheat oven to 350°F (175°C). Lightly grease a 9x13 inch baking dish.

2. In a large bowl, whisk together the eggs, sour cream, Cheddar cheese, green chile peppers, green onion, and parsley. Mix in the corn, black beans, red pepper, and bacon bits. Transfer to the prepared baking dish.

3. Bake 30 minutes in the preheated oven, or until a knife inserted in the center of the casserole comes out clean. Serve with the fresh salsa.

Tortilla Casserole

Submitted by: **Raquel**

Makes: 12 servings

Preparation: 20 minutes

Cooking: 1 hour

Ready In: 10 hours 20 minutes

"This a great overnight brunch casserole when you have a house full of holiday guests! Serve with salsa and sour cream."

INGREDIENTS

12 (6 inch) corn tortillas

2/3 cup chopped green onions

1 (4 ounce) can sliced black olives, drained

2 (4 ounce) cans diced green chile peppers, drained

1 (4 ounce) jar diced pimento peppers, drained

8 ounces Monterey Jack cheese, shredded

8 ounces Cheddar cheese, shredded

5 eggs

2 cups milk

1 (8 ounce) jar salsa

DIRECTIONS

1. Lightly grease a 9x13 inch baking dish. Line the bottom of the dish with 4 tortillas. Sprinkle with ⅓ each of the green onions, olives, chile peppers, pimento peppers, Monterey Jack cheese, and Cheddar cheese. Repeat twice with the remaining ingredients.

2. In a large bowl, beat together eggs, milk, and salsa. Pour over the layered ingredients. Cover with plastic wrap, and refrigerate overnight.

3. Remove the casserole from refrigerator, and remove plastic wrap. Preheat oven to 350°F (175°C).

4. Bake 45 to 60 minutes in the preheated oven.

Brunch Enchiladas

Submitted by: **Darlene Blunck**

Makes: 10 servings

Preparation: 30 minutes

Cooking: 1 hour

Ready In: 9 hours 30 minutes

"Enchiladas filled with ham, vegetables and cheese and baked in a creamy egg batter."

INGREDIENTS

1 pound cooked ham, chopped

3/4 cup sliced green onions

3/4 cup chopped green bell peppers

3 cups shredded Cheddar cheese, divided

10 (7 inch) flour tortillas

5 eggs, beaten

2 cups half-and-half cream

1/2 cup milk

1 tablespoon all-purpose flour

1/4 teaspoon garlic powder

1 dash hot pepper sauce

DIRECTIONS

1. Place ham in food processor, and pulse until finely ground. Mix together ham, green onions, and green peppers. Spoon 1/3 cup of the ham mixture and 3 tablespoons shredded cheese onto each tortilla, then roll up. Carefully place filled tortillas, seam side down, in a greased 9x13 baking dish.

2. In a medium bowl, mix together eggs, cream, and milk, flour, garlic powder, and hot pepper sauce. Pour egg mixture over tortillas. Cover, and refrigerate overnight.

3. The next morning, preheat oven to 350°F (175°C).

4. Bake, uncovered, in preheated oven for 50 to 60 minutes, or until set. Sprinkle casserole with remaining 1 cup shredded cheese. Bake about 3 minutes more, or until cheese melts. Let stand a least 10 minutes before serving.

Broccoli and Cheese Brunch Casserole

Submitted by: **Linda K.**

Makes: 8 servings

Preparation: 15 minutes

Cooking: 55 minutes

Ready In: 1 hour 20 minutes

"Delicious for a brunch or weekend breakfast."

INGREDIENTS

8 ounces pork sausage

1 (10 ounce) package chopped frozen broccoli, thawed and drained

1½ cups shredded Cheddar cheese, divided

1 cup ricotta cheese

8 eggs, lightly beaten

¼ cup milk

1 teaspoon ground black pepper

½ teaspoon salt

1 roma (plum) tomato, thinly sliced

DIRECTIONS

1. Place sausage in a large, deep skillet. Cook over medium-high heat until evenly brown. Drain, crumble, and set aside.

2. Preheat oven to 350°F (175°C). Lightly grease a 7x11 inch baking dish.

3. In a bowl, mix cooked sausage, broccoli, and ½ cup Cheddar cheese. In a separate bowl, mix ½ cup Cheddar cheese, ricotta cheese, eggs, milk, pepper, and salt. Spoon the sausage mixture into the prepared baking dish. Spread the Cheddar and ricotta mixture over the sausage mixture. Sprinkle with remaining Cheddar. Arrange tomato slices on top.

4. Cover with aluminum foil, and bake 30 minutes in the preheated oven. Uncover, and bake for an additional 15 minutes. Let stand for 10 minutes before serving.

Crab Brunch Casserole

Submitted by: **Doreen**

Makes: 8 servings

Preparation: 15 minutes

Cooking: 1 hour

Ready In: 1 hour 15 minutes

"A delicious casserole - elegant enough for a Sunday brunch!"

INGREDIENTS

2 eggs, beaten

2 cups milk

2 cups seasoned croutons

8 ounces shredded Cheddar cheese

1 tablespoon dried minced onion

1 tablespoon dried parsley

1 pound fresh crabmeat

salt and pepper to taste

¼ cup grated Parmesan cheese

DIRECTIONS

1. Preheat oven to 325°F (165°C). Lightly grease a medium baking dish.

2. In large bowl, mix the eggs, milk, croutons, cheese, onion, and parsley. Stir in the crabmeat. Season with salt and pepper. Spoon into the prepared baking dish, and sprinkle with Parmesan cheese.

3. Bake 1 hour in the preheated oven, or until a knife inserted into center of the casserole comes out clean. Serve immediately.

Oklahoma Cheese Grits

Submitted by: **Mollie**

Makes: 12 servings

Preparation: 15 minutes

Cooking: 1 hour 10 minutes

Ready In: 1 hour 30 minutes

"It's a great day when my Mom serves up this Southern specialty! Cooked grits are combined with seasonings, cheese, and eggs, then baked. The eggs are the secret to light fluffy grits that melt in your mouth! You may adjust or eliminate the hot sauce to suit your taste."

INGREDIENTS

6 cups water

1½ cups quick-cooking grits, dry

¾ cup butter

1 pound processed cheese, cubed

2 teaspoons seasoning salt

1 tablespoon Worcestershire sauce

½ teaspoon hot pepper sauce

2 teaspoons salt

3 eggs, beaten

DIRECTIONS

1. Preheat oven to 350°F (175°C). Lightly grease a 9x13 inch baking dish.

2. In a medium saucepan, bring the water to a boil. Stir in grits, and reduce heat to low. Cover, and cook 5 to 6 minutes, stirring occasionally. Mix in the butter, cheese, seasoning salt, Worcestershire sauce, hot pepper sauce, and salt. Continue cooking for 5 minutes, or until the cheese is melted. Remove from heat, cool slightly, and fold in the eggs. Pour into the prepared baking dish.

3. Bake 1 hour in the preheated oven, or until the top is lightly browned.

Overnight Blueberry French Toast

Submitted by: **Karan Cox**

Makes: 10 servings

Preparation: 15 minutes

Cooking: 1 hour 15 minutes

Ready In: 10 hours

"This is a very unique breakfast dish. Good for any holiday breakfast or brunch, it's filled with the fresh taste of blueberries, and covered with a rich blueberry sauce to make it a one of a kind."

INGREDIENTS

12 slices day-old bread, cut into 1 inch cubes

2 (8 ounce) packages cream cheese, cut into 1 inch cubes

1 cup fresh blueberries

12 eggs, beaten

2 cups milk

1 teaspoon vanilla extract

⅓ cup maple syrup

1 cup white sugar

2 tablespoons cornstarch

1 cup water

1 cup fresh blueberries

1 tablespoon butter

DIRECTIONS

1. Lightly grease a 9x13 inch baking dish. Arrange half the bread cubes in the dish, and top with cream cheese cubes. Sprinkle 1 cup blueberries over the cream cheese, and top with remaining bread cubes.

2. In a large bowl, mix the eggs, milk, vanilla extract, and syrup. Pour over the bread cubes. Cover, and refrigerate overnight.

3. Remove the bread cube mixture from the refrigerator about 30 minutes before baking. Preheat the oven to 350°F (175°C).

4. Cover, and bake 30 minutes. Uncover, and continue baking 25 to 30 minutes, until center is firm and surface is lightly browned.

5. In a medium saucepan, mix the sugar, cornstarch, and water. Bring to a boil. Stirring constantly, cook 3 to 4 minutes. Mix in the remaining 1 cup blueberries. Reduce heat, and simmer 10 minutes, until the blueberries burst. Stir in the butter, and pour over the baked French toast

allrecipes tried & true slow cooker & casserole | brunch

Apple Raisin French Toast Strata

Submitted by: **Terrie**

Makes: 12 servings

Preparation: 20 minutes

Cooking: 45 minutes

Ready In: 3 hours 15 minutes

"A simple but elegant way to make breakfast fast. Put together the night before, and bake while you're in the shower. Serve with lots of extra maple syrup! You may also add extra raisins if you wish."

INGREDIENTS

1 (1 pound) loaf cinnamon raisin bread, cubed

1 (8 ounce) package cream cheese, diced

1 cup diced peeled apples

8 eggs

2½ cups half-and-half cream

6 tablespoons butter, melted

¼ cup maple syrup

DIRECTIONS

1. Coat a 9x13 inch baking dish with cooking spray. Arrange ½ of the cubed raisin bread in the bottom of the dish. Sprinkle the cream cheese evenly over the bread, and top with the apples. If you like extra raisins, add them now. Top with remaining bread.

2. In a large bowl, beat the eggs with the cream, butter, and maple syrup. Pour over the bread mixture. Cover with plastic wrap, and press down so that all bread pieces are soaked. Refrigerate at least 2 hours.

3. Preheat oven to 325°F (165°C).

4. Bake 45 minutes in the preheated oven. Let stand for 10 minutes before serving.

Creme Brulee French Toast

Submitted by: **Sandi**

Makes: 6 servings

Preparation: 20 minutes

Cooking: 40 minutes

Ready In: 9 hours

"Very rich French toast - can be made ahead of time."

INGREDIENTS

½ cup unsalted butter

1 cup packed brown sugar

2 tablespoons corn syrup

6 (1 inch thick) slices French bread

5 eggs

1½ cups half-and-half cream

1 teaspoon vanilla extract

1 teaspoon orange brandy

¼ teaspoon salt

DIRECTIONS

1. Melt butter in a small saucepan over medium heat. Mix in brown sugar and corn syrup, stirring until sugar is dissolved. Pour into a 9x13 inch baking dish.

2. Remove crusts from bread, and arrange in the baking dish in a single layer. In a small bowl, whisk together eggs, half and half, vanilla extract, orange brandy, and salt. Pour over the bread. Cover, and chill at least 8 hours, or overnight.

3. Preheat oven to 350°F (175°C). Remove the dish from the refrigerator, and bring to room temperature.

4. Bake uncovered 35 to 40 minutes in the preheated oven, until puffed and lightly browned.

French Toast Souffle

Submitted by: **Betty**

Makes: 12 servings

Preparation: 20 minutes

Cooking: 30 minutes

Ready In: 9 hours 20 minutes

"This is a scrumptious casserole of bread, cream cheese, eggs, and milk. Tastes just like regular French toast but it's made the night before and baked in the oven. This is not really sweet so you might like more maple syrup with it."

INGREDIENTS

10 cups white bread cubes

1 (8 ounce) package lowfat cream cheese, softened

8 eggs

1½ cups milk

⅔ cup half-and-half cream

½ cup maple syrup

½ teaspoon vanilla extract

2 tablespoons confectioners' sugar

DIRECTIONS

1. Place bread cubes in a lightly greased 9x13 inch baking pan.

2. In a large bowl, beat cream cheese with an electric mixer at medium speed until smooth. Add eggs one at a time, mixing well after each addition. Stir in milk, half and half, maple syrup, and vanilla until mixture is smooth. Pour cream cheese mixture over the bread; cover, and refrigerate overnight.

3. The next morning, remove souffle from refrigerator, and let stand at room temperature for 30 minutes. Meanwhile, preheat oven to 375°F (190°C).

4. Bake, uncovered, for 30 minutes in the preheated oven, or until a knife inserted in the center comes out clean. Sprinkle with confectioners' sugar, and serve warm.

Maple Syrup Casserole Made in Heaven

Submitted by: **Dawn Dehart**

Makes: 8 Servings

Preparation: 15 minutes

Cooking: 45 minutes

Ready In: 9 hours

"This recipe has been passed down for years, and is tried and true to be a break-fast pleaser for the old, and the young, and everyone in between. You can not go wrong! As a Home Ec teacher, I have satisfied many a teacher and student belly with this scrumptious French Toast."

INGREDIENTS

1 (1 pound) loaf day-old French bread

1 (8 ounce) package cream cheese

2 cups milk

12 eggs

2 cups maple syrup

DIRECTIONS

1. Slice the loaf of French bread into about 25 slices, and set aside. In a large bowl, whisk together the eggs, milk, and maple syrup.

2. Place enough bread slices in the bottom of a 9x13 inch baking dish to cover. Drop 2 teaspoons or so of cream cheese onto each slice. You do not need to spread the cheese. Repeat layering with bread slices and cream cheese until the dish is filled to the top. Slowly pour the egg mixture over the layers, so it doesn't run over the sides. Cover, and refrigerate 8 hours or overnight.

3. The next morning, preheat the oven to 375°F (190°C).

4. Bake casserole for 45 minutes, or until set and golden brown.

dessert

No need for a fuss with these easy baked desserts! The hard part is the wait while the house fills with the aroma of sweet success. Showcase the best fruits of the season in a fruity cobbler or crisp. Don't throw away that stale bread - give it a second chance as a stunning bread pudding. These easy desserts are all served from the baking dish, making them extra convenient for bringing along to any festive occasion.

Rhubarb Strawberry Crunch

Submitted by: **Michelle Davis**

Makes: 18 servings

Preparation: 15 minutes

Cooking: 45 minutes

Ready In: 1 hour

"Ever wonder what to do with that big rhubarb plant in the garden?? This is your answer."

INGREDIENTS

1 cup white sugar

3 tablespoons all-purpose flour

3 cups sliced fresh strawberries

3 cups diced rhubarb

1½ cups all-purpose flour

1 cup packed brown sugar

1 cup butter

1 cup rolled oats

DIRECTIONS

1. Preheat oven to 375 °F (190°C).

2. In a large bowl, mix white sugar, 3 tablespoons flour, strawberries, and rhubarb. Place the mixture in a 9x13 inch baking dish.

3. Mix 1½ cups flour, brown sugar, butter, and oats until crumbly. You may want to use a pastry blender for this. Crumble on top of the rhubarb and strawberry mixture.

4. Bake 45 minutes in the preheated oven, or until crisp and lightly browned.

Cherry Crisp

Submitted by: **Holly**

Makes: 6 servings

Preparation: 10 minutes

Cooking: 30 minutes

Ready In: 55 minutes

"A truly incredible dessert! It's just soooo good and really easy to make. Everyone always raves about it and asks me for the recipe when I make it. Wonderful served with whipped topping or ice cream. Great for vegans!"

INGREDIENTS

1 (21 ounce) can cherry pie filling

1/2 cup all-purpose flour

1/2 cup rolled oats

2/3 cup brown sugar

3/4 teaspoon ground cinnamon

3/4 teaspoon ground nutmeg

1/4 cup chopped pecans

1/3 cup melted margarine

DIRECTIONS

1. Preheat oven to 350°F (175°C.) Lightly grease a 2 quart baking dish. Pour pie filling into the dish, and spread evenly.

2. In a medium bowl, mix together flour, oats, sugar, cinnamon, and nutmeg. Mix in melted margarine. Spread over pie filling, and sprinkle with chopped pecans.

3. Bake in the preheated oven for 30 minutes, or until topping is golden brown. Allow to cool 15 minutes before serving.

Triple Berry Crisp

Submitted by: **Polly Giebler**

Makes: 18 servings

Preparation: 20 minutes

Cooking: 40 minutes

Ready In: 1 hour

"This is a wonderful berry crisp. I use a triple berry mixture of raspberries, blackberries, and blueberries, but just one works well too! My family loves it! Serve it with whipped cream and it looks great."

INGREDIENTS

1½ cups fresh blackberries

1½ cups fresh raspberries

1½ cups fresh blueberries

4 tablespoons white sugar

2 cups all-purpose flour

2 cups rolled oats

1½ cups packed brown sugar

1 teaspoon ground cinnamon

½ teaspoon ground nutmeg

1½ cups butter

DIRECTIONS

1. Preheat oven to 350°F (175°C).

2. In a large bowl, gently toss together blackberries, raspberries, blueberries, and white sugar; set aside.

3. In a separate large bowl, combine flour, oats, brown sugar, cinnamon, and nutmeg. Cut in butter until crumbly. Press half of mixture in the bottom of a 9x13 inch pan. Cover with berries. Sprinkle remaining crumble mixture over the berries.

4. Bake in the preheated oven for 30 to 40 minutes, or until fruit is bubbly and topping is golden brown.

Maple Apple Crisp

Submitted by: **Crystal**

Makes: 8 servings

Preparation: 20 minutes

Cooking: 35 minutes

Ready In: 55 minutes

"Tender apples kissed with maple syrup and covered in a rich, crunchy topping. Very easy, and tastes great!! My fiance loves when I make this dessert."

INGREDIENTS

5 apples - peeled, cored, and sliced

3/4 cup maple syrup

1/2 cup all-purpose flour

1/2 cup rolled oats

1/2 cup brown sugar

1 pinch salt

1/2 cup butter, softened

DIRECTIONS

1. Preheat oven to 375 °F (190°C).

2. Place apples in an 8x8 inch baking dish. Toss apples with syrup. In a separate bowl, mix together flour, oats, sugar, and salt. Cut in butter until mixture is crumbly. Sprinkle mixture evenly over apples.

3. Bake in the preheated oven for 35 minutes, until topping is golden brown. Serve warm or at room temperature.

Nana's Apple Crisp

Submitted by: **Keri C.**

Makes: 8 servings

Preparation: 15 minutes

Cooking: 50 minutes

Ready In: 1 hour 5 minutes

"Very quick and easy recipe! Delicious with vanilla ice cream!"

INGREDIENTS

6 tart apples - peeled, cored, and sliced

½ cup butter, melted

1 cup all-purpose flour

1 cup white sugar

1 cup quick-cooking oats

2 tablespoons ground cinnamon, divided

¼ cup butter, cut into pieces

DIRECTIONS

1. Preheat oven to 350°F (175°C).

2. Place apples in a 9x13 inch baking dish. In a bowl, mix melted butter, flour, sugar, oats, and 1 tablespoon cinnamon to form a crumbly mixture. Sprinkle over apples. Dot with remaining ¼ cup butter, and sprinkle with remaining 1 tablespoon cinnamon.

3. Bake 50 minutes in the preheated oven, until lightly browned and apples are tender.

Cranberry Apple Casserole

Submitted by: **Christine Hanson**

Makes: 8 servings

Preparation: 5 minutes

Cooking: 40 minutes

Ready In: 45 minutes

"Super simple side dish, perfect for holiday or everyday meals. Goes great with chicken, turkey, ham, or pork. Can also double as a not-too-sweet dessert when served with ice cream or whipped cream."

INGREDIENTS

1 (21 ounce) can apple pie filling

1 (16 ounce) can whole berry cranberry sauce

1/4 cup butter, softened

1 1/2 cups rolled oats

3/4 cup brown sugar

DIRECTIONS

1. Preheat oven to 350°F (175°C).

2. Combine apple pie filling and cranberry sauce in a shallow baking dish.

3. In a medium bowl, mix the butter, oats, and brown sugar until crumbly. Sprinkle evenly over the fruit mixture.

4. Bake in the preheated oven for 40 minutes, or until browned and crisp.

Apple, Cranberry, and Pear Crisp

Submitted by: **Barb Y**

Makes: 8 servings

Preparation: 15 minutes

Cooking: 45 minutes

Ready In: 1 hour

"This is a variation of the traditional Apple Crisp that I dreamed up one day when I didn't have enough apples, and there were pears in the fruit bowl, and leftover toasted hazelnuts from something else. We love it. Cranberries can be substituted with raisins or dried cherries. Comice pears taste best with this recipe."

INGREDIENTS

2 Rome Beauty apples - peeled, cored, and cubed

2 Comice pears - peeled, cored, and cubed

½ cup dried cranberries

1 tablespoon all-purpose flour

2 tablespoons honey

1½ tablespoons lemon juice

½ cup all-purpose flour

½ cup packed brown sugar

½ cup quick cooking oats

¼ cup ground walnuts

½ cup butter

DIRECTIONS

1. Preheat oven to 375°F (190°C). Lightly grease an 8 inch baking dish.

2. Mix the apples, pears, cranberries, 1 tablespoon flour, honey, and lemon juice in the prepared dish.

3. In a bowl, mix ½ cup flour, brown sugar, oats, walnuts, and butter to the consistency of coarse crumbs. Sprinkle loosely over the fruit mixture.

4. Bake 45 minutes in the preheated oven, or until brown and crisp on top.

Rhubarb Cobbler

Submitted by: **Jill Saunders**

Makes: 9 servings

Cooking: 20 minutes

Ready In: 20 minutes

"My family really loves this recipe. Hope you have good luck with it!"

INGREDIENTS

¾ cup white sugar

2 tablespoons cornstarch

4 cups chopped rhubarb

1 tablespoon water

1 tablespoon butter, diced

1 teaspoon ground cinnamon

1 cup all-purpose flour

1 tablespoon white sugar

1½ teaspoons baking powder

¼ teaspoon salt

¼ cup butter

¼ cup milk

1 egg, beaten

2 tablespoons white sugar

DIRECTIONS

1. Preheat oven to 400°F (200°C). Lightly grease a 9 inch square baking dish.

2. In a saucepan, mix ¾ cup sugar and cornstarch. Stir in the rhubarb and water. Bring to a boil. Cook and stir for 1 minute. Transfer to the prepared baking dish. Dot with butter, and sprinkle with cinnamon.

3. In a medium bowl, sift together flour, 1 tablespoon sugar, baking powder, and salt. Cut in the butter until the mixture resembles coarse crumbs.

4. In a small bowl, mix the milk and egg. Add all at once to dry ingredients, stirring just to moisten. Drop by teaspoonfuls on top of the rhubarb mixture. Sprinkle with sugar.

5. Bake for 20 minutes in the preheated oven, until crisp and lightly browned.

Strawberry Cobbler II

Submitted by: **Michael**

Makes: 8 servings

Preparation: 30 minutes

Cooking: 45 minutes

Ready In: 1 hour 15 minutes

"It is very good when served warm with whipped cream."

INGREDIENTS

½ cup white sugar

1 tablespoon cornstarch

1 cup water

3 cups sliced fresh strawberries

2 tablespoons margarine

1 cup all-purpose flour

¼ cup packed dark brown sugar

1½ teaspoons baking powder

½ teaspoon salt

3 tablespoons butter

¾ cup half-and-half cream

¼ cup margarine

¼ cup packed dark brown sugar

DIRECTIONS

1. Preheat oven to 400°F (200°C) Grease a 2 quart baking dish with margarine.

2. In a medium saucepan, combine sugar, cornstarch, water, and strawberries. Cook over medium heat, stirring constantly, until thick and hot. Pour mixture into the prepared baking dish. Dot with 2 tablespoons margarine.

3. In a bowl, combine flour, ¼ cup brown sugar, baking powder, and salt. Blend in the 3 tablespoons butter. Stir in cream. Mixture should be soft. When you spoon dough onto the berries, it will probably sink to the bottom. Just try to spread as well as you can. Don't worry, it comes out good.

4. Bake for about 20 to 25 minutes in the preheated oven. When the cobbler is almost done, mix the ¼ cup margarine and ¼ cup brown sugar, and heat them in a saucepan or in the microwave (whichever is easier for you). When the topping is heated, brush it on the top of the cobbler and bake for another 5 to 10 minutes.

Old Fashioned Peach Cobbler

Submitted by: **Eleta**

Makes: 18 servings

Preparation: 30 minutes

Cooking: 1 hour 10 minutes

Ready In: 2 hours 10 minutes

"I was searching for a peach cobbler recipe that reminded me of the yummy dessert I ate as a young girl in Southeast Missouri. No shortcuts here. Fresh peaches and homemade crust...but worth every minute! Absolutely delicious served warm with vanilla ice cream! Never any leftovers with this dessert!"

INGREDIENTS

2½ cups all-purpose flour

3 tablespoons white sugar

1 teaspoon salt

1 cup shortening

1 egg

¼ cup cold water

3 pounds fresh peaches - peeled, pitted, and sliced

¼ cup lemon juice

¾ cup orange juice

½ cup butter

2 cups white sugar

½ teaspoon ground nutmeg

1 teaspoon ground cinnamon

1 tablespoon cornstarch

1 tablespoon white sugar

1 tablespoon butter, melted

DIRECTIONS

1. In a medium bowl, sift together the flour, 3 tablespoons sugar, and salt. Work in the shortening with a pastry blender until the mixture resembles coarse crumbs. In a small bowl, whisk together the egg and cold water. Sprinkle over flour mixture, and work with hands to form dough into a ball. Chill 30 minutes.

2. Preheat oven to 350°F (175°C). Roll out half of dough to 1/8 inch thickness. Place in a 9x13 inch baking dish, covering bottom and halfway up sides. Bake for 20 minutes, or until golden brown.

3. In a large saucepan, mix the peaches, lemon juice, and orange juice. Add ½ cup butter, and cook over medium-low heat until butter is melted. In a mixing bowl, stir together 2 cups sugar, nutmeg, cinnamon, and cornstarch; mix into peach mixture. Remove from heat, and pour into baked crust.

4. Roll remaining dough to a thickness of ¼ inch. Cut into half-inch-wide strips. Weave strips into a lattice over peaches. Sprinkle with 1 tablespoon sugar, and drizzle with 1 tablespoon melted butter.

5. Bake in preheated oven for 35 to 40 minutes, or until top crust is golden brown.

Peach Berry Cobbler

Submitted by: **Amy Posont**

Makes: 8 servings

Preparation: 15 minutes

Cooking: 35 minutes

Ready In: 50 minutes

"The fresh taste of peaches combined with fresh blueberries, warm and slightly spicy, under a crunchy, soft biscuit topping. Serve warm with ice cream. Cinnamon may be used in place of nutmeg."

INGREDIENTS

1 cup all-purpose flour

½ cup white sugar

1½ teaspoons baking powder

½ cup milk

¼ cup butter, softened

¼ cup packed brown sugar

1 tablespoon cornstarch

½ cup cold water

3 cups fresh peaches - peeled, pitted and sliced

1 cup fresh blueberries

1 tablespoon butter

1 tablespoon lemon juice

2 tablespoons coarse granulated sugar

¼ teaspoon ground nutmeg

DIRECTIONS

1. Preheat oven to 350°F (175°C).

2. In a medium bowl, stir together flour, ½ cup white sugar, and baking powder. Mix in milk and ¼ cup butter until smooth.

3. In a medium saucepan, stir together the brown sugar, cornstarch, and water. Mix in the peaches and blueberries. Cook and stir over medium heat until thick and bubbly. Mix in 1 tablespoon butter and lemon juice. Continue cooking until the butter melts. Pour into a 1½ quart ungreased baking dish. Evenly spoon batter in mounds over the hot fruit. In a small bowl, mix the coarse sugar and nutmeg, and sprinkle over the batter.

4. Place the baking dish on a shallow baking pan in the preheated oven. Bake cobbler for about 35 minutes, or until bubbly and a toothpick inserted into the crust comes out clean.

Fresh Fruit Cobbler

Submitted by: **Victor**

Makes: 6 servings

Preparation: 30 minutes

Cooking: 30 minutes

Ready In: 1 hour

"Never use more than 1 quart of fruit. Only use fresh fruit for this recipe. Any variation will work! I usually do use sweetened peaches and lightly sugared berries, but this is optional. Serve warm with cream, ice cream, or whipped cream."

INGREDIENTS

1 cup sliced fresh peaches

3/4 cup peeled, cored and sliced apple

3/4 cup peeled, cored and sliced pear

1/2 cup blueberries

1/2 cup pitted and sliced cherries

1/2 cup pitted and sliced plums

1 egg

3/4 cup white sugar

1/4 cup milk

1 cup all-purpose flour

1 teaspoon baking powder

1/2 teaspoon salt

1/2 teaspoon vanilla extract

2 tablespoons butter, melted

DIRECTIONS

1. Preheat oven to 350°F (175°C). Grease a 2 quart baking dish.

2. Arrange the peaches, apple, pear, blueberries, cherries, and plums in the prepared baking dish. In a medium bowl, beat egg, sugar, and milk. In a separate bowl, sift together flour, baking powder, and salt; stir into the egg mixture. Stir in vanilla and melted butter. Cover the fruit with the batter mixture.

3. Bake 30 minutes in the preheated oven. Cobbler should be bubbly and lightly browned. Serve warm.

Apple Pecan Cobbler

Submitted by: **Lori Smith**

Makes: 8 servings

Preparation: 30 minutes

Cooking: 55 minutes

Ready In: 1 hour 25 minutes

"This is an excellent cobbler to make in the fall when the weather starts to turn cooler."

INGREDIENTS

4 cups thinly sliced apples

½ cup white sugar

½ teaspoon ground cinnamon

½ cup chopped pecans

1 cup all-purpose flour

1 cup white sugar

1 teaspoon baking powder

¼ teaspoon salt

1 egg, beaten

½ cup evaporated milk

⅓ cup butter, melted

¼ cup chopped pecans

DIRECTIONS

1. Preheat oven to 325°F (165°C). Generously grease a 2 quart baking dish.

2. Arrange apple slices in an even layer in the baking dish. In a small bowl, mix together ½ cup sugar, cinnamon, and ½ cup pecans. Sprinkle mixture over apples.

3. In a medium bowl, mix together flour, 1 cup sugar, baking powder, and salt. In a separate bowl whisk together egg, evaporated milk, and melted butter. Pour milk mixture into flour mixture all at once, and stir until smooth. Pour mixture over apples, and sprinkle top with ¼ cup pecans.

4. Bake in the preheated oven for 55 minutes.

Pineapple Cobbler

Submitted by: **Kristina**

Makes: 10 servings

Preparation: 15 minutes

Cooking: 30 minutes

Ready In: 45 minutes

"A cobbler like a pineapple upside down cake."

INGREDIENTS

½ cup butter

1 cup self-rising flour

1 cup white sugar

1 cup milk

1 (15 ounce) can pineapple chunks, drained

½ cup brown sugar

1 (4 ounce) jar maraschino cherries, halved

DIRECTIONS

1. Preheat oven to 400°F (200°C). In a 9x13 inch baking dish, melt the butter in the oven.

2. In a medium bowl, stir together flour, white sugar, and milk until smooth. Pour batter into the prepared dish.

3. In a separate bowl, toss pineapple with brown sugar until fruit is well coated. Drop pineapple mixture by spoonfuls into the batter. Sprinkle with cherries.

4. Bake 30 minutes in the preheated oven, until golden.

Zucchini Cobbler

Submitted by: **Beverly**

Makes: 18 servings

Preparation: 20 minutes

Cooking: 40 minutes

Ready In: 1 hour

"Let's say you have an abundance of zucchini, but you're fresh out of apples. You can sneak this on the kids and they'll never know."

INGREDIENTS

5 cups zucchini - peeled, seeded, and chopped

½ cup fresh lemon juice

¾ cup white sugar

1 teaspoon ground cinnamon

½ teaspoon ground nutmeg

4 cups all-purpose flour

1½ cups white sugar

1½ cups butter, chilled

1 teaspoon ground cinnamon

DIRECTIONS

1. Preheat oven to 375°F (190°C). Coat a 9x13 inch baking dish with cooking spray.

2. Place zucchini and lemon juice in a medium saucepan. Cook, covered, over medium-low heat, stirring occasionally, for about 15 minutes, or until tender. Stir in ¾ cup sugar, 1 teaspoon cinnamon, and nutmeg. Simmer 1 minute longer, remove from heat, and set aside.

3. In a large mixing bowl, combine flour and 1½ cups sugar. Cut in butter until the mixture resembles coarse crumbs. Stir ½ cup crumb mixture into zucchini mixture. Press half the remaining crumb mixture into the prepared pan. Spread zucchini evenly over crust. Crumble remaining crumb mixture over zucchini, and sprinkle with 1 teaspoon cinnamon.

4. Bake in the preheated oven for 35 to 40 minutes, or until golden and bubbly.

Bread Pudding

Submitted by: **Missi**

Makes: 12 servings

Preparation: 10 minutes

Cooking: 1 hour

Ready In: 1 hour 10 minutes

"This is one of my favorite desserts. The sauce makes the dessert! I don't use raisins, but a lot of people like to add them in."

INGREDIENTS

3 cups bread cubes

4 cups scalded milk

¾ cup white sugar

1 tablespoon butter

½ teaspoon salt

4 eggs, lightly beaten

1 teaspoon vanilla extract

1 cup white sugar

½ cup butter

½ cup heavy cream

1 teaspoon vanilla extract

DIRECTIONS

1. Preheat oven to 350°F (175°C).

2. Butter an 8x8 inch glass baking dish. Soak bread in hot milk for five minutes. Stir in ¾ cup sugar, 1 tablespoon butter, salt, eggs, and 1 teaspoon vanilla. Pour into the baking dish.

3. Line a roasting pan with a damp kitchen towel. Place baking dish on towel inside roasting pan, and place roasting pan on oven rack. Fill roasting pan with boiling water to reach halfway up the sides of the baking dish. Bake for 60 minutes. Cool on wire rack.

4. While pudding cools, combine 1 cup sugar, ½ cup butter, cream, and 1 teaspoon vanilla in a large saucepan. While stirring, bring to a boil. Reduce heat to low, and stir 3 minutes more. Spoon over warm bread pudding.

Chocolate Banana Bread Pudding

Submitted by: **Gabrielle**

Makes: 8 servings

Preparation: 20 minutes

Cooking: 1 hour

Ready In: 1 hour 20 minutes

"A local restaurant served a version of this recipe. I went crazy over it and decided to create my own. It's great served warm or cold."

INGREDIENTS

4 eggs

2 cups milk

1 cup white sugar

1 tablespoon vanilla extract

4 cups cubed French bread

2 bananas, sliced

1 cup semisweet chocolate chips

DIRECTIONS

1. Preheat oven to 350°F (175°C). Grease a 9x5 inch loaf pan.

2. In a large mixing bowl, mix eggs, milk, sugar, and vanilla until smooth. Stir in bread, bananas, and chocolate chips, and let rest 5 minutes for bread to soak. Pour into prepared pan.

3. Line a roasting pan with a damp kitchen towel. Place loaf pan on towel inside roasting pan, and place roasting pan on oven rack. Fill roasting pan with water to reach halfway up the sides of the loaf pan. Bake in preheated oven for 1 hour, or until a knife inserted in the center comes out clean.

Gramma's Apple Bread Pudding

Submitted by: **Meshel**

Makes: 8 servings

Preparation: 15 minutes

Cooking: 50 minutes

Ready In: 1 hour

"This bread pudding is the ultimate in comfort food from Gramma's kitchen. It is great for using up bread and apples. Enjoy!"

INGREDIENTS

PUDDING

4 cups soft bread cubes

¼ cup raisins

2 cups peeled and sliced apples

1 cup brown sugar

1¾ cups milk

¼ cup margarine

1 teaspoon ground cinnamon

½ teaspoon vanilla extract

2 eggs, beaten

VANILLA SAUCE

¼ cup white sugar

¼ cup brown sugar

½ cup milk

½ cup margarine

1 teaspoon vanilla extract

DIRECTIONS

1. Preheat oven to 350°F (175°C). Grease a 7x11 inch baking dish.

2. In a large bowl, combine bread, raisins, and apples. In a small saucepan over medium heat, combine 1 cup brown sugar, 1¾ cups milk, and ¼ cup margarine. Cook and stir until margarine is melted. Pour over bread mixture in bowl.

3. In a small bowl, whisk together cinnamon, ½ teaspoon vanilla, and eggs. Pour bread mixture into prepared dish, and pour egg mixture over bread.

4. Bake in preheated oven 40 to 50 minutes, or until center is set and apples are tender.

5. While pudding is baking, mix together sugar, ¼ cup brown sugar, ½ cup milk, and ½ cup margarine in a saucepan. Bring to a boil, then remove from heat, and stir in 1 teaspoon vanilla. Serve over bread pudding.

Apple Betty

Submitted by: **Barbara Milam**

Makes: 8 servings

Preparation: 30 minutes

Cooking: 45 minutes

Ready In: 1 hour 15 minutes

"Everyone always raves about this pie. You don't have to make pie crust! You can control the sweetness by the amount of streusel topping you use."

INGREDIENTS

4 cups thinly sliced apples

1/4 cup orange juice

3/4 cup all-purpose flour

1 cup white sugar

1/2 teaspoon ground cinnamon

1/4 teaspoon ground nutmeg

1 pinch salt

1/2 cup butter

DIRECTIONS

1. Preheat oven to 375°F (190°C). Lightly grease a 9 inch pie plate.

2. Mound sliced apples in the pie plate. Sprinkle with orange juice.

3. In a medium bowl, mix the flour, sugar, cinnamon, nutmeg, and salt. Cut in butter until the mixture resembles coarse crumbs. Scatter over the apples.

4. Bake in preheated oven for 45 minutes. Serve warm.

Applesauce Noodle Kugel

Submitted by: **Angela Creighton**

Makes: 12 servings

Preparation: 20 minutes

Cooking: 1 hour 10 minutes

Ready In: 1 hour 30 minutes

"Tender noodles are stirred with a comforting blend of margarine, sour cream, egg substitute, sugar, lemon juice, vanilla extract, chunky applesauce, and raisins. Bake over a light sprinkling of graham cracker crumbs and top with cinnamon for a sweet treat."

INGREDIENTS

1 (16 ounce) package wide egg noodles

1 cup reduced fat margarine

1/2 cup fat free sour cream

1 1/2 cups egg substitute

2 cups white sugar

1 teaspoon lemon juice

1 teaspoon vanilla extract

1/2 (16 ounce) jar applesauce

1/4 cup raisins

1/4 cup graham cracker crumbs

1 teaspoon ground cinnamon, or to taste

DIRECTIONS

1. Preheat oven to 350°F (175°C). Coat a 9x13 inch baking dish with cooking spray. Bring a large pot of lightly salted water to a boil. Cook noodles in boiling water for 8 to 10 minutes, or until al dente. Drain.

2. In a large bowl, mix together margarine, sour cream, egg substitute, sugar, lemon juice, vanilla extract, and applesauce. Stir in noodles and raisins.

3. Spread graham cracker crumbs on the bottom of the prepared dish. Pour the noodle mixture over the crumbs. Sprinkle top with cinnamon.

4. Bake 45 to 60 minutes in the preheated oven, or until set. Cover with foil if it browns too quickly.

Virginia Apple Pudding

Submitted by: **Dorothy and Kathy Keizer**

Makes: 6 servings

Preparation: 10 minutes

Cooking: 30 minutes

Ready In: 40 minutes

"This is a wonderful old family recipe served warm, topped with vanilla ice cream."

INGREDIENTS

½ cup butter, melted

1 cup white sugar

1 cup all-purpose flour

2 teaspoons baking powder

¼ teaspoon salt

1 cup milk

2 cups chopped, peeled apple

1 teaspoon ground cinnamon

DIRECTIONS

1. Preheat oven to 375 °F (190°C).

2. In a small baking dish, combine butter, sugar, flour, baking powder, salt, and milk until smooth.

3. In a microwave-safe bowl, combine apples and cinnamon. Microwave until apples are soft, 2 to 5 minutes. Pour apples into the center of the batter.

4. Bake in the preheated oven 30 minutes, or until golden.

Old-Fashioned Rice Pudding

Submitted by: **Juanita**

Makes: 6 servings

Preparation: 15 minutes

Cooking: 2 hours 30 minutes

Ready In: 2 hours 45 minutes

"This pudding turns out in a lovely custard texture. A great balm for those seeking a return to some of the old-fashioned foods of their youth! We like it best because it is oven-baked and not made on the stove top."

INGREDIENTS

2 eggs, beaten

4 cups milk

1/2 cup white sugar

1/2 cup uncooked white rice

1 tablespoon butter

1 teaspoon vanilla extract

1/2 cup raisins (optional)

1/8 teaspoon ground nutmeg

DIRECTIONS

1. Preheat oven to 300°F (150°C). Grease a 2 quart baking dish.

2. Beat together the eggs and milk. Stir in white sugar, uncooked rice, butter, vanilla extract, raisins, and nutmeg. Pour into prepared pan.

3. Bake for 2 to 2½ hours in the preheated oven. Stir frequently during the first hour.

Dump Cake V

Submitted by: **Barbara**

Makes: 18 servings

Preparation: 15 minutes

Cooking: 1 hour

Ready In: 1 hour 15 minutes

"This recipe for dump cake is more like a cobbler type dessert than it is a cake. I serve it in a bowl with whipped cream, ice cream, or frozen whipped topping. It is quick to prepare and it is delicious."

INGREDIENTS

1 (21 ounce) can cherry pie filling

1 (20 ounce) can crushed pineapple, drained

1 (18.25 ounce) package yellow cake mix

1 cup margarine, melted

1 cup flaked coconut

½ cup chopped walnuts

DIRECTIONS

1. Preheat oven to 350°F (175°C). Lightly grease a 9x13 inch baking dish.

2. In the prepared dish, layer the cherry pie filling and the drained pineapple. Sprinkle the dry cake mix over the top, covering evenly. Pour the melted margarine over the cake mix, and sprinkle the top with the coconut and chopped walnuts.

3. Bake 50 to 60 minutes in the preheated oven, until browned and bubbly.

recipe contributors

Linda K. 235
Linda McCann 224
Lindsay 161
Lisa 70
Lisa Bromfield 168
Lisa Humpf 123
Lisa Rosenkrans 226
Lori Smith 258
Lorrie Starks 221
Lynn Eberle 165
Mandy19j 96
Marge 33
Margo Collins 41
Maria 202
Marilyn G. 142
Mary 128
Mary Lee Jones 188
Mary Moon 115
Maryanne 209
Maureen 28
Melanie 231
Melanie Burton 136
Melissa Wardell 220
Merri 35
Meshel 263
Michael 254
Michele O'Sullivan 87, 203
Michelle Davis 246
Micki Stout 121

Mindy McCoy 183
Missi 261
Mollie 237
Monika Polly 111
Mouse 208
Muse 223
Nancy (i) 43
Nancy (ii) 116
Nicki 25
Paula 201, 204
Peggy 39
Perri Pender 86
PJ 84
Polly Giebler 248
Randi DeWeese 170
Raquel Davis 187
Raquel (ii) 233
Rayna Jordan 157
Rebecca 140
Rebecca Miller 182
Rhonda S. 37
Rose Small 153
Rosie 117
Rosie T. 42
Roxanne E Chan 232
Ruthie Crickmer 198
Sandi 240
Sarah Jane 119
Christopher Kruse 73

Scotty 76
Seth Henderson 52
Sharon 189
Sharon Pruitt 138
Shirley 94
Mike Purll 50
Sierra 59
Sue 63
Sue (i) 122
Sue (ii) 169
Sue Ann Buck 110
Sue Schuler 219
Susan 152
Susan Madsen 227
Suzanne Cook 196
Suzanne (ii) 77
Tami 134
Tanya 91
Teri Denlinger 97
Terrie 239
Terrilyn Singleton 88
Terry Covert 143
Tim Pipher 200
Tom Quinlin 194
Tracy Mantell 99
Victor 257
Wendy 49

index

credits

the staff at allrecipes

Jennifer Anderson	Jim Kreyenhagen
Barbara Antonio	Kala Kushnik
Mary Ashenden	William Marken
Justin Bross	Elana Miller
Emily Brune	Carrie Mills
Scotty Carreiro	Bill Moore
Sydny Carter	Todd Moore
Jill Charing	Yann Oehl
Jeff Cummings	Lesley Peterson
Kirk Dickinson	Alicia Power
Steven Hamilton	Carl Trautman
Blanca Hernandez	Esmee Williams
Tim Hunt	Krista Winjum
Jenni Johns	Sarah Young
Richard Kozel	A.K. Zebdi

thanks

The staff would like to thank the following people whose comments and feedback have made this a better book: Brenda Hunt, David Quinn, and Hillary Quinn.

the allrecipes tried & true series

Our *Tried & True* cookbooks feature the very best recipes from the world's greatest home cooks! Allrecipes.com, the #1 recipe website, brings you the "Best of the Best" dishes and treats, selected from over 24,000 recipes! We hand-picked only recipes that have been awarded 5-star ratings time and time again, so you know every dish is a winner.

Current titles include:

Allrecipes Tried & True Favorites; Top 300 Recipes

Filled with the best-loved recipes from Allrecipes.com - these have all won repeated standing ovations from millions of home cooks and their families, intrepid eaters and picky kids alike.

Allrecipes Tried & True Cookies; Top 200 Recipes

Enjoy the world's best cookie recipes and invaluable baking tips and tricks that will turn anyone into an expert on preparing, decorating and sharing cookies. With over 230 cookie recipes, you'll find tried and true recipes for all your old favorites, and lots of new favorites too!

Allrecipes Tried & True - Quick & Easy; Top 200 Recipes

Great-tasting meals in minutes! This cookbook features delicious dishes that can be prepared in minutes. Discover the joys of cooking without spending hours in the kitchen!

Allrecipes Tried & True - Thanksgiving & Christmas; Top 200 Recipes

So many treasured holiday memories are made around the table! For Thanksgiving dinners, family breakfasts, Christmas parties and more, rely on this collection of beloved favorites that have stood the test of time.

Allrecipes Tried & True - All Season Grilling & BBQ; Top 200 Recipes

America's best-loved grilling and barbeque recipes have been pulled together for this one-of-a-kind collection featuring Allrecipes best-of-the-best recipes for sizzling steaks, juicy chicken, sensational seafood, zesty sauces and marinades, simple salads, side dishes and more.

Allrecipes *Tried & True* cookbooks are available at select bookstores, by visiting our website at http://www.allrecipes.com, or by calling 206-292-3990 ext. #239. Watch for more *Tried & True* cookbooks to come!

Allrecipes.com · 400 Mercer St., Suite 302 · Seattle, WA 98109 USA · Phone: (206) 292-3990